In Touch with Healing

UNA KROLL

GW00367238

BBC BOOKS

For Betty and all sevikas like her

Una Kroll was born in London in 1925, had a cosmopolitan upbringing in London, Paris and Riga, and became a medical doctor in 1951. She married an American Episcopalian priest in 1957 and they worked in England, Liberia and Namibia before her four children were old enough to go to school. She and her family then settled in England. She spent most of her working life as a general medical practitioner, but has also worked in a psychiatric hospital and as a community medical officer.

In 1970 she became a deaconess-worker of the Church of England. She has been actively involved in the Christian healing ministry since then. When her husband died in 1987 she decided to retire from medical practice a̶n̶d̶ move to Wales. Since 1988 she has been a deacon of the Church in Wales and has lived with members of the Society of the Sacred Cross at Tymawr Convent. She is presently seeking membership of the Society.

© Una Kroll 1991
ISBN 0 563 36319 3
Published by BBC Books
a division of BBC Enterprises Limited
Woodlands, 80 Wood Lane, London W12 0TT
First published 1991
Set in Linotron Palatino by Phoenix Photosetting, Chatham, Kent
Cover printed by Clays Ltd, St Ives PLC
Printed and bound in Great Britain by Clays Ltd, St Ives PLC

Acknowledgements

I thank all who have been patients, friends and colleagues for their share in my explorations into healing, especially those who have asked awkward questions, refused to let me get away with woolly thinking and sent me back to seek guidance from the Holy Spirit.

In particular, I thank John Polkinghorne for reading part of Chapter Three. He had reservations about my use of analogy, but kindly corrected some errors in my thinking and clarified my use of language. I thank all the people whose stories I have told, most of whom I know personally, but some of whom I have only met through other books. I am grateful to my community for allowing me to do this work, to Martha Caute and Ann Richardson of the BBC who made visits to our convent and who supplied invaluable material for me to use. I thank all my children and friends who encouraged me.

I thank Harcourt, Brace and World Inc. for permission to quote from *The Complete Poems of Cavafy*.

I return thanks to God for the stamina to write this book, to St John of the Cross under whose patronage it was written, and to my spiritual director whose encouragement I needed at a crucial time in its genesis.

Contents

Introduction

Look to your health; and if you have it, praise God, and
value it next to a good conscience; for health is the second
blessing that we mortals are capable of; a blessing that
money cannot buy.

Izaak Walton (1593–1683)[1]

A few months ago I was walking up Victoria Street in
London. I had just passed Westminster Cathedral when I
was seized with a severe stabbing pain in my left groin. I
gasped, limped into a doorway, and pretended to look at the
goods on display while I tried to sort out what had happened.
The pain seemed to disappear as soon as I stood still. My
doctor's diagnostic mind immediately took over and came up
with a reassuring answer. If the pain ceased when I stopped
moving it couldn't be anything too serious. I patted myself on
the back for this astute insight, waited for a few minutes, and
then attempted to move on. The pain returned with an uncomfortable ferocity. I discovered that I could walk on slowly,
though with a limp.

I was due to meet a friend at Westminster Abbey and I
wasn't going to let a stupid pain defeat me. So I gritted my
teeth and went on, persuading myself that I was just over-
reacting to a pulled muscle. I arrived at Westminster Abbey
and met my friend. We had arranged to have a short holiday
together and were going to drive back to the convent in Wales
where I live.

By the time we reached my parked car I was sweating with
pain. I sank thankfully into the driver's seat. The pain abated. I
breathed a sigh of relief, assured my friend that I was perfectly
all right to drive and got on with it.

1

'What happened?' she said.

'Oh, I don't know. I expect I've pulled a muscle. It'll pass.'

Thousands of people would probably have given the same answer. They react, as I did, by denying the reality of their pain. When they can't do that, they ignore its possible significance.

Four hours later we got out of the car. As soon as I put my weight on to my left leg it collapsed under me. I staggered inside. One of the nuns greeted me kindly.

'What's happened?' she said.

'Nothing. I've just pulled a muscle. I'll be all right in the morning. I'll go to bed early.'

Sure enough the pain eased when I got into bed. But in the morning it was there again as soon as I put my legs on to the floor. I felt nauseated at once.

I had not been used to pain of that sort. For most of my life I had been possessed of good health, Izaak Walton's 'second blessing'. So it was quite a shock to find myself so limited in mobility. Moreover I was feeling quite ill by this time, and worried lest I should have a really serious disease. That morning I knew that I must do something about helping myself.

First, I wanted to be cured, that is to say I wanted to return to the state of ease and well-being that I had enjoyed before that pain in my hip had started. I wanted the pain to go away. I wanted to be able to walk freely again. So, naturally enough, I thought I would go to the doctor and find out what was wrong and get some treatment.

There was nothing wrong in wanting to be cured. That is what most of us want when we fall ill. At the same time I was, even then, aware of the possibility that it might not be curable. The pain could be due to severe arthritis of the hip joint, or a silent fracture or a secondary cancer. At my age all those were statistical possibilities. Or I might have contracted some other disease, like a bone infection, which would take a long time to heal. If I couldn't be cured, could I expect some improved function, some lessening of the pain in my joint? Or was it going to settle into a chronic disability? Already, before I had even

2

entered my general practitioner's waiting room, I had rehearsed all the various gloomy possibilities in my mind. My growing anxiety increased my awareness of the pain and I decided that as soon as I had been to see the doctor I would also seek some healing.

Being cured and being healed are not at all the same thing. Healing is a much wider concept, as I hope to show. To ask for healing is to ask to be made whole, that is to say to reach a state of well being in body, mind and spirit that can triumph over a continuing sickness in one aspect of oneself. Being healed is to be set free from limitations so that one can fulfil one's potential as a human being in relation to others. We cannot always be cured, but we can always be healed.

I knew very well that my doctor might be able to cure me, but she would not necessarily have the skill or time to heal me. For that I would have to accept some responsibility myself, and I might well need the help of a healer or a healing prayer group.

I decided to go to the doctor first. She examined me and, as my joint moved reasonably well when I was lying down, she was not greatly worried. She advised me to rest as much as I could, prescribed some pain-killers and suggested that I lose weight.

I left the consulting room feeling a bit foolish. Had I experienced as much pain as I thought? Had I worried unnecessarily? I put all thoughts of serious illness out of my mind and decided I did not need any healing either.

I did what I was told to do, but the pain persisted. X-rays showed some arthritis in the hip. I was told that the pain would probably fluctuate. If the tablets stopped working, or I grew worse, I might benefit from a hip replacement operation. At this stage I began to realise that I needed to be healed even if I wasn't going to be cured in the way I had hoped.

I had always valued my fitness. Now that it had apparently disappeared so rapidly I wondered if I had done anything to cause it. If I had, then my general practitioner would not necessarily be able to help me. I might need to find out how I

3

had contributed to my condition and ask God to heal me of those things I had done, or not done, which might have affected my susceptibility to illness.

Over the next few weeks I found quite a lot of things wrong with my lifestyle. In joining a community of nuns I had left a job that I loved. I had some worries about how my grown-up children were feeling about what I was doing. I was having some 'teething troubles' learning to be a novice. I had bottled up my feelings instead of talking openly about them. I had ignored some small warning signs. Now that I was ill I had time to deal with some of these difficulties. I do not believe that God caused the illness in order to force me to think about my lifestyle, but I do believe that God helped me discern those aspects of my life that needed putting right.

I could not do this work alone. Some people can heal themselves, but I can't. I need other people's support and help. I found the help that I needed quite quickly and easily. I have a very simple faith. I know that God loves me and is always close to me. I am able to trust his appointed means for healing. So I found someone to talk to. I also asked for healing prayer and the laying on of hands. In one sense nothing happened; that is to say I wasn't cured. In another sense everything happened, for I noticed subtle changes in my own attitude towards myself. God's peace and assurance came to me through those talks and through the healing prayers. I knew that I was becoming more whole through my illness.

I firmly believe that all healing comes from God. That belief underlies all that I say in this book, but I am also aware that God can and does act through many different people in many different ways. Christians don't have a monopoly on healing; there are many different kinds of healers. What matters most is that people who need healing should be able to find individuals and groups of people with the integrity to help them.

This book is written with three aims: to discuss what healing is and how it takes place; to outline some of the ways in which an individual might begin to search for the right kind of help;

and finally to show how good it is to take responsibility for our own health, to value and preserve it.

My own personal search for health is not finished, nor will my personal story end with the writing of this book. The search for healing will not end for any of us until we come to the final healing of death. But I have made some progress. I have accepted the likelihood that I shall continue to suffer some pain and disability from my diseased hip joint. I have not lost hope of a cure. I think it is important to retain this hope, even though I know the chances are small. But I have focused on the search for wholeness and I believe that I have made progress towards being healed. Some of the ways in which that has happened will be described further on in this book. In the meantime I should like to explore in more detail what we mean by healing and how it occurs.

CHAPTER ONE

Uncovering Some Truths About Healing

> We cannot separate our attitude to health from our
> attitude to life.
>
> *David Jenkins, Bishop of Durham*[1]

Some time in the early 1970s a shyly smiling man walked into a room full of medical doctors. He took off his glasses, looked around, and began his lecture with the words: 'There is no such thing as health.' I was there to hear that statement and can remember feeling amused. It was, I thought, one of David Jenkins' typical opening remarks, calculated to jolt an audience into listening to what he had to say. It was a characteristic that was to remain with him when he became Bishop of Durham in 1984. At the time of that lecture, however, he was an academic theologian with a deep interest in, and knowledge of, the National Health Service.

I settled down to listen, or rather to argue with him inside my head. After all, I and all the other doctors in that room were employees of the National Health Service. We certainly thought we knew what health was. We even went so far as to say that we knew when a person was healthy and when they were not.

A New Insight Into Health

Most of the doctors who listened to David Jenkins that day would have supposed that most people started life as healthy individuals. As doctors, one of our greatest joys was examining a newborn infant and being able to turn to the mother and say: 'You've got a lovely healthy baby'. What we were doing when we said that was equating health with normality. We would, for instance, say that a baby was healthy or normal, if he or she had certain facial features, ten fingers and ten toes, all the usual body openings and could be easily identified as a boy or a girl.

All the doctors present had certain criteria by which they could judge whether an individual was normal or abnormal, healthy or unhealthy. That idea – namely that health exists, that it is possible to define it by reference to an average norm which you have arbitrarily chosen – was what the future Bishop of Durham was challenging. It was a challenge that I was resisting, but when I listened more carefully to what he was saying I began to understand his point of view.

That lecture changed my attitude towards health quite dramatically. David Jenkins was trying to broaden our horizons so that we could stop thinking of health as something we have until we are ill. Instead he was urging us to think of it as something we work towards all through our lives. Later on he wrote about the same thing in an introduction to a book on health by Dr James McGilvray (a man who was instrumental in setting up the Christian Medical Commission which works to improve health care in poorer countries):

> We cannot separate our attitude to health from our attitude to
> life. That is why you cannot, and, indeed, must not define
> health. Like life it is an open and as yet undefinable, because as
> yet unfulfilled, possibility . . . Health is thus a value and a
> vision word which has both to be brought constantly down to
> earth and to be related persistently to a promise, an aim and a
> hope which lies ahead and above us.[2]

I mention David Jenkins' views at this very early stage because I want to show how much our concepts about health matter. They largely determine the ways in which we approach healing. If people seek healing, are they asking to go back to what they once were, or are they looking 'persistently to a promise, an aim and a hope which lies ahead and above us'?

There is, I believe, no single answer to this question. It is not really possible to say that one way of thinking about health is right and another wrong. With some illnesses, we will simply want to go back to the way we felt before we were ill. If, for instance, I catch a streaming head cold, I know that I don't need to do very much about it, other than take simple home-made remedies and wait for the cold to abate so that I can say I have recovered my health. I am treating health as something I once had, which now needs to be recovered. The chances are that most of us do think about health this way most of the time.

At other times, however, when the malaise is more complex and more persistent, or when we grow older, we may find ourselves thinking about health as something we are working towards. There are occasions when we are left with some disability, and we realise that we are never going to return to what we were before. At such times we have to start seeing health as a state of well-being which can encompass some permanent handicap or disability.

David Jenkins had given a new insight, at least for me, into the meaning of healing. In the years since he made his speech I have seen many of his ideas becoming more widely accepted. We are part of a historical process and, as I look back over the history of the healing arts, I see that there have been other significant shifts of attitude towards healing during my own lifetime. There has, for instance, been a revival of interest in some of the ancient healing arts and the role of faith in healing. Many people have turned away from technological medicine in favour of alternative systems of health care. There has been a resurgence of interest in the role of faith in healing. These shifts of attitude merit attention.

The Recovery of Ancient Healing Arts

When I look back at the history of the healing arts I am, of course, aware of some of the great landmarks in curative medicine, and of the debt we owe to scientists throughout the ages who have made marvellous discoveries which have bene-fited all creation. But it is not they whom I want to remember now. It is the countless men and women whose names do not appear in medical history books.

There have always been people who have developed

healing skills. They have made use of herbs, leaves and tree barks, for medicines; they have prescribed homeopathic remedies; they have developed skills in observation and diagnosis; they have discovered liniments, soothing oils and massage for muscular ailments. They have set bones skilfully, and manipulated joints. They have developed acupuncture and acupressure.[3] They have provided different diets for almost every condition under the sun. They have passed on the art of deep relaxation. They have even used ecstasy to release powerful emotions which could not be channelled in any other way. They have used hypnosis, auto-suggestion, listening, talking, counselling in therapeutic ways.

All these skills are very old indeed. Many of them come from ancient civilisations like those of China and India. Some of them – like Ayurvedic healing (an Indian system of medicine) and transcendental meditation[4] – almost disappeared under the impact of Western technology during the early part of this century. Since the early 1960s, however, when people in Western countries began to experience profound disillusionment with allopathic medicine,[5] many of these ancient arts have been recovered and are enjoying considerable success.

I have lived in small villages in two different African countries and have seen many of these skills in use. They had not been learned from books or imported from afar. They had developed out of centuries of experience, and although by Western standards some of the treatments seemed primitive, or even harmful, there was much to be learnt from these indigenous healers.

Many of these healing arts are handed down within families, but from very early times it has been customary to learn such skills by apprenticeship. Professional healers carry considerable authority in any small community; they attract a considerable amount of covert criticism, and can be rather alarming, since they often appear to be able to read one's thoughts. Certainly the witch doctors and native medicine men in my African villages possessed these skills, which they used both to enhance their own reputations and to gain power over people. They also used them for the benefit of the very sick people whom they treated.

In the last thirty years, since I left Africa, there has been a resurgence of interest in alternative therapies. Some of them have been recovered, others revamped to suit Western appetites.[6] Their reappearance has been part of a reaction against technology.

The Rise of Alternative Ways of Healing

In Western Europe, America and Australia alternative therapies of every kind now abound. Vast numbers of people follow special diets to preserve their health or combat various diseases (ranging from arthritis to behavioural disorders, multiple sclerosis and cancer). Many people consult acupuncturists, reflexologists, osteopaths, herbalists and aromatherapists. Some seek out colour therapy; others are fascinated by auras and their meaning. Some people embrace Tai Chi, a Chinese form of calisthenics. Others become experts in yoga.[7] Astrologers and clairvoyants are in demand, and their predictions are seen by many as ways of maintaining good health and fortune. This move away from technology is significant. It represents a shift away from scientifically proven therapies to therapies which rely on personal relationships. There is a reaction against the relatively impersonal five- or ten-minute consultation with a technologist and a movement towards a consultation with a particular person who is willing to spend considerable time with each client. These alternative practitioners may also use unfamiliar techniques which often induce a client to trust in a seemingly useless piece of equipment such as a mysterious looking black box, or ritual, such as that which initiates a course in transcendental meditation.

Uncovering the Role of Faith in Healing

The move away from technlogy has also resulted in a greater interest in the role of faith. A person's faith in a healer may be quite unconnected with any religious belief. It may be faith in spirits, as is often the case in those African countries where the people are animists. It may be faith in God. It may be faith in the souls of dead people, as in the spiritualist tradition of 'spirit guides'. Or it may be faith in one of the great monotheistic religions – Judaism, Christianity or Islam. Faith is a suspension of disbelief, a handing over of oneself to another person or soul, or to God, in the knowledge that they represent a power to heal.

The Christian churches have always known about the role of faith in healing. The New Testament is full of stories about Jesus who 'did many signs and wonders', and healed many who came to him with divers diseases.[8] His apostles and early disciples sometimes cured people of their infirmities and diseases in exactly the same way as their master had done. Those who were sick were encouraged to call for the Church elders, who would pray over them, lay healing hands on them and often anoint them with oil.

Throughout the history of the Church that kind of personal ministry has continued. The writings of the early Fathers, for instance, are studded with references to healing.[9] Miracles have occurred and pilgrimages to shrines have often been rewarded by the recovery of physical health. Christians have always tended the sick. Nevertheless, from post-apostolic times onwards, people's confidence in the healing ministries of the Church gradually declined as scientific knowledge increased.[10] By the middle of the nineteenth century there was little expectation that people would be cured of their diseases by prayer and related practices. Even anointing with oil was associated with preparation for death rather than a return to well-being. All that was to change and, interestingly enough, the changes were accelerated by some remarkable women.

St Bernadette of Lourdes (1844–79) was one of those people who make visible changes that are already happening in God's world. Sceptical scientists and clerics tried to discount the healings that took place at Lourdes after Bernadette's visionary experiences had uncovered a previously hidden spring of clear water. When drunk or bathed in, this water seemed to have remarkable healing properties. Some people were cured of

11

their diseases; far more received healings and blessings. Although only a handful of cures have been attested by scientists as miraculous, healings (in the sense of moving towards wholeness) frequently occur at Lourdes, and it still attracts thousands of pilgrims and sick people every year.[11]

A few years later St Thérèse of Lisieux (1873–97) died of tuberculosis. She had written a remarkable account of her spiritual journey which was posthumously circulated and quickly reached a wide audience. Within a very short time of her death people began to pray to her and many healings were recorded. St Thérèse was canonised in 1925 and is still one of the great figures in the history of healing.[12]

When Dorothy Kerin (1889–1963) was healed instantly on 18 February 1911, in what appeared to be the final stages of generalised tuberculosis, her doctors were amazed. Her general practitioner, Dr Norman, had fully expected that Dorothy would die. When he was called to the house on 19 February he could scarcely believe his eyes. The day before, Dorothy had been prostrate in bed, where she had been confined for the previous five years. She had been semi-conscious and emaciated. The young woman who ran to greet him at the door that morning was 'plump and well and smiling'. He 'lifted up his hands in astonishment, saying, "Can it be possible that this is the girl which I LEFT DYING?" Recovering somewhat from the shock, he then examined her and pronounced her well and healthy.'

Dorothy had experienced a vision on the night of 18 February. She had heard a voice saying, 'Dorothy, your sufferings are over. Get up and walk.'[13] A few years later Dorothy Kerin, an Anglican, began a remarkable healing ministry of prayer and the laying on of hands. Thousands of people were helped by her. She encountered much suspicion and hostility in the early years, but she also attracted many good and influential people to her side and eventually did much to help the Church of England develop its healing ministry. She founded a residential healing centre at Burrswood in Groombridge, Kent, in 1948.

By the time she died in 1963 Dorothy Kerin was widely respected. Her great contribution came from her realisation that medicine and religion were not opposed to each other, but could work together for the benefit of sick human beings. That tradition is still carried on at Burrswood today. The healing centre is in a beautiful house set in spacious grounds. Patients who are ill are attended by specialists, resident doctors and nurses in a well-equipped nursing home. The chaplains are part of the team. They visit anyone who wants to talk to them, and, together with the warden (who is a doctor) and other staff members, they hold regular healing services in the chapel. Those who are too ill to attend are able to hear the services in their rooms and to receive healing there.

Although some of the people who go to Burrswood are very ill, others are not. Many people just need a rest, some space to think, or someone to consult about a problem. These visitors can stay in a different part of the house, enjoy the lovely gardens, read, rest, join in community prayers, receive counselling and participate in any of the activities in the house.

Dorothy Kerin's idea of medical staff, ministers of religion and intercessors working together for the benefit of all who need healing has spread to many other centres. Each has its own special emphasis. One that I know well is at St Marylebone Church in London.

This venture was started by Christopher Hamel Cooke. He began his working life as a parish priest and while he was Vicar of St Mark's, Coventry, he studied for a Diploma in Pastoral Studies in Birmingham. That course re-oriented his ministry and he became deeply involved in the work of the Samaritans. After some years he was appointed as Rector of St Marylebone Parish Church. He was given a vision of it as a healing centre. And, obedient to that vision, he converted the huge crypt into a place where many different healing ministries could happily co-exist. Now there is a holistic general medical practice; and music therapy and acupuncture are available. Counselling and prayer ministries also continue to grow and expand. This centre started from nothing and has grown into a mighty place.[14]

Other developments in Christian healing ministry came out of the Pentecostal renewal movements which began in America in the late nineteenth century.[15] These renewal movements focused on the gifts of the Holy Spirit that St Paul wrote about in his letter to the Corinthians. These include gifts of wisdom, knowledge and faith; gifts of healing, the working of miracles, prophecy, discernment of spirits, speaking in tongues and interpreting tongues. Since the mid-twentieth century there has been a revival of interest in charismatic healing, that is healing by the direct intervention of the Holy Spirit through gifts from God which are imparted to individuals and groups of individuals.[16] Americans like Agnes Sandford, Kathryn Kuhlman and Jo Kimmel, all of whom attracted thousands of people to their healing services, feature in all the healing literature of that time.[17]

By the 1960s many people were disillusioned with technological medicine. The healing ministries of individuals were authenticated by experience. All over the world priests of all denominations began to take the healing ministry more seriously. In England, George Bennet, an Anglican priest, established a healing ministry at Crowhurst in Battle and wrote many books.[18] In 1974 Father Francis MacNutt, at that time an American Roman Catholic Dominican priest, wrote a book called *Healing* which had a very wide circulation. It, and his other books, won many people over to the charismatic healing ministries.[19] There has since been a rapid rise in the literature about healing, and the names of people like David Watson,[20] John Wimber,[21] Colin Urquhart[22] and Trevor Deering have become very well known.

In the middle of this century Anglican priests, like Father Gilbert Shaw (1886–1967),[23] began their deliverance ministries of prayer and exorcism. These ministries are concerned with freeing people from bondage to sin, fear and evil impulses (within themselves or emanating from outside influences such as evil people or demons). The increase in such ministries over the last twenty or thirty years is probably related to the rise of interest in the occult and satanism, which are seen as ways in

14

which human beings can gain power over others. Although the dramatic aspects of deliverance ministries are somewhat unhelpful at times, the role of spiritual evil in the genesis of illness cannot, I believe, be discounted.[24] Much work remains to be done in this field before any of us can appreciate the importance that deliverance ministries have in the healing work of the whole Church.

In 1958 an Archbishops' Commission on Healing published its findings. It took a very cautious line on both charismatic and spiritual healing and suggested that healing was generally best left to health care professionals.[25] As if in reaction to that report, the healing ministries of all the mainstream churches have proliferated ever since.

In recent years the focus has changed from individual ministry to group work. The clergy and great healing figures no longer have the monopoly of healing. Instead, healing services are becoming quite a common feature of church life in many places. Lay people as well as clergy usually take part in such services and healing is seen as something everyone is involved in. Many churches support small groups of lay people who come together for prayer, mutual support and the laying on of hands. We are all starting to see the naturalness of praying to God, the author of all healing, as well as taking the sensible, practical steps of visiting a doctor or surgeon. We are beginning to understand a little about how these kinds of ministries work.[26]

Uncovering the Role of Relationships in Healing

Another aspect of healing is seen at work in ministries which largely rely on relationships as a way of healing disease. When I was a young doctor working in England in the 1950s, older professional colleagues tended to discount the effects of emotions, personal problems and stress on patients. By the time I retired from active practice in 1987, attitudes had changed a great deal, and the psychological aspects of health and healing were much better understood, even in a society where technology is still dominant. I have, in my own lifetime,

seen a shift of attitudes among doctors, associated professionals and patients that has had quite marked effects on
Western European and American society.

We are, I believe, beginning to appreciate the value of
listening, counselling and good pastoral care. People are not as
fearful of psychology and psychiatry as they once were. They
are more willing to accept the help of trained counsellors and
there is some evidence that counselling skills are permeating
society to such an extent that we are no longer so dependent
on so-called experts. Ordinary men and women are beginning
to assimilate the wisdom of these experts into their own lives
and to respond with wisdom gained from their own
experience.[27]

Uncovering the Role of Social Factors in Healing

Lastly, I must mention another change in emphasis that has
occurred during this century. This change has largely come
about though the increasing awareness of many Christians
and humanists that social evils and poor health are closely
related. Agencies like the Salvation Army in the UK have
highlighted the link between poverty, overcrowding and
social diseases; while bodies such as the World Health Organisation, OXFAM, UNICEF and CAFOD have researched the effects
of poverty in Third World countries. People like the much-
respected Bob Lambourne,[28] Michael Wilson,[29] James
McGilvray and the Christian Medical Commission of the World
Council of Churches[30] have demonstrated that more lives can
be saved in Third World countries (and other impoverished
communities which still exist in affluent countries) by training
local people, particularly women, in the principles of good diet
and hygiene. In parts of the world where hunger, thirst and
poor nutrition are responsible for so many deaths of children
and young people, the provision of clean water, good home-
grown food and simple medical remedies will do more to
eradicate certain diseases than the establishment of an expen-
sive technological hospital which can only reach a very limited
number of people.[31] These changes in attitude are gradually

16

getting through to those responsible for the development of national health services in the world.

In this book I have only been able to sketch the bare outlines of the history of all kinds of healing ministries. My view is that of someone who began life as a sceptic, trained in Western technological medicine, and only gradually came to understand the power of the spiritual to change the material. I have never seen a dramatic cure that could be described as miraculous – the kind of miracle that has occurred during pilgrimages to Lourdes – but I have seen much evidence that suggests that the invisible spiritual powers and energies of God and God's human agents are effective in healing sick people. For many years now I have used my knowledge as a doctor of medicine together with my faith as a Christian in my own work. I have unhesitatingly turned to the spiritual ministry of the Church to which I belong, as well as making use of the skills of medically trained doctors, psychiatrists, counsellors and trained listeners. I have also encouraged people to find their healing from sources other than myself and in recent years I have begun to understand that all sick people have a responsibility for co-operating with God in healing themselves. This applies as much to myself as it does to the people I meet in the healing worlds of medicine and religion.

Before turning to some of the practical aspects of healing I want to focus again on the meaning of words like wholeness, disease and healing itself.

CHAPTER TWO

Wholeness, Disease and Healing

> When we rejoice in our fullness, then we can part with
> our fruits with joy.
>
> *Rabindranath Tagore (1861–1941)[1]*

WHOLENESS

It is always easy to look up the meaning of a word in a dictionary, but far harder to understand it. *The Shorter Oxford English Dictionary* tells us that the words wholeness and heal have the same root. To be whole is to be a complete entity, an undivided unit, an object, organism or person in sound condition, a living being in good health. Clearly the word wholeness has many meanings; I want to explore some of those meanings in relation to health.

Wholeness in Objects of Beauty

> A thing of beauty is a joy for ever;
> Its loveliness increases; it will never
> Pass into nothingness; but still will keep
> A bower quiet for us, and a sleep
> Full of sweet dreams, and a health and quiet
> > breathing.
> *John Keats (1795–1821)[2]*

In my family home there are three treasured works of art. All of them are quite small and all are, in their own way, quite perfect. Together they tell me something important about wholeness, about what makes something a complete entity, an undivided unit, a wholesome object.

The first is a picture of a river running through a deep gorge. It was crafted by an unknown Soviet artist from sculpted marble pieces. Each piece is unique in colour, size and shape. Each piece is designed to fit closely with its neighbours. It must have taken the artist many hours of painstaking labour to produce such a beautiful work of art. The whole is made up of many different parts and yet each part is a work of art in its own right. If one of those individual pieces of marble had been missing or chipped the wholeness of the scene would have been marred.

My second treasure is a picture of two Spanish women. It is made from leather. On one of the women the artist has gouged out some of the leather to depict an open-weave shawl. Those holes give the picture its character. Without them the portrait of the two friends would lose something precious.

The third work of art is a hand-woven piece of cloth made up of many strands of different-coloured wool. The work is rough; it is uneven; it is flawed; and yet it glows with beauty. Every time I look at it I remember seeing the artist at work in a sheltered workshop. She was a middle-aged woman with physical and mental disabilities which made it impossible for her to live independently, or to earn her living through paid employment. Whereas some people could weave a piece of cloth of this kind in an hour or two, and a machine could make it in five minutes, this work took her many weeks to complete. It was woven out of love and suffering, and it draws out my vision to meet hers.

These three examples tell me a little about the ways in which the separate elements in a work of art can contribute to its essential unity. I know very well, however, that they cannot completely describe wholeness in living creatures. For that, I need to look at the way time plays its part in organisms.

Wholeness in Living Organisms

Flower in the crannied wall,
I pluck you out of the crannies,
I hold you here, root and all, in my hand,

Little flower – but *if* I could understand
What you are, root and all, and all in all,
I should know what God and man is.
    Alfred, Lord Tennyson (1809–1892)[3]

I remember making a thirty-day silent retreat some years ago. The aim of the retreat was to rejoice in God's goodness and to seek God's purposes for our future way of life and service. One day, in the middle of this month's silence and seclusion in North Wales, I went for a long walk. On the way back I found a tiny plant crammed tight into a small crack in an old stone wall. I could not bear to pluck it out of its home, but I remembered Tennyson's poem and mused long upon the flower's wonderful drive towards life, and the perfect timing that had brought me there just when I needed to see it in its full beauty and maturity.

It is obvious that any living thing will go through different phases during its lifetime. It will be true to the rhythms inherent in its being. Take a plant, for instance: as a seed or a bulb it is whole in one way; once the seed germinates and the roots are growing it has a different standard against which its completeness can be measured. A healthy seed will put out strong roots and shoots; in time the slowly maturing plant will break through the surface of the ground and produce flowers and fruit, before it completes its life cycle and dies. This rhythm of germination, growth, maturity and death is common to all living beings, and their wholeness consists in fulfilling the purpose for which they have been created.

The tiny plant I had seen clinging to life reminded me that I cannot regard any living thing as whole, or healthy, unless I look at it in the context of its nature and its life cycle. This suggests that aging and death should be seen as part of healthy life, rather than something that goes against it.

What is true of plants is equally true of animals, including human beings. Here the importance of time in the rhythmic cycle of life and death is illustrated by the long, slow growth from childhood into mature adulthood. It can be as healthy for someone to grow old gracefully as it would be unhealthy for them to force their body to do things that a developing child can do quite easily. The writer of the book of Ecclesiastes knew very well that 'for everything there is a season, and a time for every matter under heaven.'[4] At the end of a long list of events which he considers timely the writer says:

> I have seen the business that God has given to everyone to be busy with. He has made everything suitable for its time; moreover he has put a sense of past and future into their minds, yet they cannot find out what God has done from the beginning to the end.[5]

The Harmonies of Wholeness

> Love alone is capable of uniting living beings in such a way as to complete and fulfil them, for it alone takes them and joins them by what is deepest in themselves . . .
>
> Teilhard de Chardin (1881–1955)[6]

I have tried to indicate that a whole living creature can consist of innumerable separate parts, including some absent bits and some flaws. Its wholeness has to be considered in relation to the stage it has reached in its life cycle. Yet that is not enough. An organism must be in harmony with itself in a number of different ways if it is to be considered whole or healthy. Yet that is not enough either. A living creature must also be in harmony with its environment if it is to be fully itself. A cactus is created by God to withstand drought; its natural habitat is the desert. A porpoise is a sea creature; it will only thrive in the water. Mature human beings are so adaptable that they can live almost anywhere in the world, but they cannot survive birth and infancy without other human beings to care for them. Indeed, good and happy relationships are essential to us throughout our lives and I do not think we can be said to be whole without them. With these relationships, we can be whole even if we are deformed, handicapped, diseased or dying.

To speak of harmony is to evoke memories of wonderful

21

pieces of music we have heard, or the song of a thrush or a nightingale in summer. But what does harmony mean in human life? Can it embrace disharmony? I think it can, up to a point. It's a question of balance. When any organism is functioning well it finds its balance in nature. If a plant receives enough nutrients from the soil, enough rainwater, and has a strong enough life-force, it will grow into beautiful maturity. Everything in its environment is right; so it is right too. For human beings this kind of balance is harder to achieve because we are individuals with complex minds and temperaments.

Physical well-being is important to us, but it is not enough. It is the harmonising of the different facets of our personalities that is vital to our well-being. Moreover, these personalities have to blend in with other members of our families and communities. Since we are social beings, we need to live in an environment where we are enriched by our differences. At the same time we also need to like each other enough to be able to survive the disharmonies that inevitably occur between people who live together. In a healthy community or society such differences can be absorbed, but if the discordant elements are too prominent – either in one's own personality or in one's family or community – then the balance is destroyed and the personality or community is precipitated into disharmony and disease. When the balance is preserved, however, it is possible to progress towards even greater harmony within society.

This point of view is well expressed in a statement dating from 1944, when some young South Africans met to form the African Youth League. One of them, a man called Anton Lembede, contrasted some white people's attitudes towards the universe with those of Africans. He wrote:

The white man regards the universe as a gigantic machine hurtling through time and space to its final destruction: individuals in it are but tiny organisms with private lives that lead to private deaths: personal power, success and fame are the absolute measures of values, the things to live for. This outlook on life divides the universe into a host of little individual entities

WHOLENESS, DISEASE AND HEALING

which cannot help being in constant conflict thereby hastening the approach of the hour of their final destruction.

> The African . . . regards the universe as one composite whole; an organic entity, progressively driving towards greater harmony and unity, whose individual parts exist merely as interdependent aspects of one whole, realising their fullest life in the corporate life whose communal contentment is the absolute measure of values.[7]

Forty-five years ago, very few people outside black Africa, or another Third World country, would probably have had that kind of vision of society. However times have changed, and I think fewer of us in affluent societies would now feel fulfilled ourselves if we did not believe the world offered that same chance of fulfilment to others. This desire to see all things made whole has influenced all those in the caring professions and many who work in the field of healing.

Finding Our Wholeness in God

So then, is it enough to be in harmony with oneself, with other people and with one's environment? For some people it may be. But I need to be in tune with something greater than myself, some ideal which draws me towards a goal I can imagine but not yet see. And I am not at all unusual in this.

Human beings have a deep desire for fulfilment and many of us express this desire through religion. God comes to people in many ways, through many cultures and traditions. I have the deepest respect for all religious belief but I have to say that my own faith as a Christian is of the utmost importance to me, so much so that I naturally hope other people will find the beginnings of their own wholeness through contact with God. God is the agent of all healing, often half glimpsed and unrecognised, but always there. Many of our healings are partial, steps on the way towards eventual wholeness. So we can rejoice in what we are given now without ceasing from our quest for the one in whom we shall find our ultimate fulfilment.

The kind of satisfying wholeness I am talking about can be found in Jesus Christ who says 'Follow me', and who invites us to search for our true health. Often the search for that kind of wholeness starts from the point of our need, from the experience of disease.

DISEASE

To talk of diseases is a sort of Arabian Nights entertainment.
Sir William Osler (1849–1919)[8]

Sir William Osler was a famous English physician who described many illnesses in minute detail, to the great benefit of his colleagues and their patients. I certainly know what he means about the 'thousand and one' diseases we encounter in the world – one simply doesn't know where to start. So I'm not going to focus initially on particular diseases. Instead, I want to think about disease in general, which is rather different. If we are going to talk about healing as being restored to functional health, or as attaining to wholeness, then we have to know what we need to be healed from. Disease is that state which alerts us to our need of healing. We therefore have to understand something of its meaning, both in its broadest sense, and also in its particular manifestations.

Dis-ease in Creation

Broadly speaking, disease can be defined as an absence of ease. That is so wide a definition that it might almost describe the entire human condition. And, indeed, some Christians would say that original sin is a disease from which we cannot be rescued, save by Christ's loving act of atonement. They would contend that it was primal disobedience to God which caused all suffering and dis-ease. Left to ourselves, we are so out of step with God that we are lost, subject to irredeemable suffering and the annihilation of death. It is only through Christ that we can be rescued, redeemed, healed, saved.

In its most extreme form this idea leads to the view that disease is the inevitable result of sin, and that all diseases are therefore related to sin. Indeed, this is a very deep-seated belief among many people. As a medical doctor I have heard many patients say: 'What have I done to deserve this?' Or, of a friend or relative, 'Why has God punished her?' Sadly, it is often very difficult to convince them that God doesn't send thunderbolts of disease from on high to punish them, however horrendous their sin. That is not to say that human beings have no responsibility for damaging their health. They evidently do.

My own belief is that suffering and sin are the consequences of creation having been made in such a way that separation from God is possible. Angelic disobedience initiated that fission, and primal sin does separate us from the wholeness of God, but divine goodness and mercy towards everything in creation ensure that such separation is only temporary. In my view, wholeness and salvation are part of God's purpose for creation. My whole being reverberates to those wonderful words of St Paul's:

> For the creation waits with eager longing for the revealing of the children of God; for the creation was subjected to futility not of its own will but by the one who subjected it, in hope that the creation itself will be set free from its bondage to decay and will obtain the freedom of the glory of the children of God.[9]

In that hope I rest.

I do not regard all sickness as due to human sin, nor do I believe that God deliberately sends diseases to punish individuals. At the same time I do think that some social diseases are the direct consequence of human wickedness and that our personal sins can contribute to our illnesses. I also think other people's wickedness – both those close at hand and those who hate us from a distance – can make us ill, especially if we know that they are projecting waves of hatred in our direction. This may upset people very much and they may become ill with the stress it imposes on them. They may, for instance, develop stomach ulcers because of their anxiety, or even have a heart attack because of their fear of a malevolent enemy.

Evil and Disease

Many people have asked whether I believe in demonic disease. The answer is yes. I do believe that malevolent spiritual entities can attack and harm living human beings. They cannot gain access to us unless we allow them to do so. Yet, through our propensity for flirting with evil, and through our frailties, we can open ourselves to cosmic evil, as St Paul said when he wrote to Christians in Ephesus telling them to:

> Put on the whole armour of God, so that you may be able to stand against the wiles of the devil. For our struggle is not against enemies of blood and flesh, but against the rulers, against the authorities, against the cosmic powers of this present darkness, against the spiritual forces of evil in the heavenly places.[10]

Yes, I believe in the wiles of the devil, even though I recognise that many people project on to him responsibilities which they should properly accept as their own. I think very few people are actually affected by contact with occult forces. Demonic sickness is extremely rare and it should never be our first thought when we fall ill. Its diagnosis is a skilled matter and should be made by medical doctors and experienced spiritual healers working together and with the afflicted person, family or community. I shall say more about this when we come to consider deliverance healing ministries.

Disease and Suffering

In speaking about some of the causes of disease and suffering I must admit that all my rational arguments tend to disappear under the impact of personal suffering. Suffering remains a profound mystery, even though I can sometimes see its possible causes in my own life. I admit that I find it very difficult to listen patiently to people who try to give me definitive answers when I am screaming at God and them because I am in physical, emotional or spiritual pain. Moreover, on a wider level, I find it very difficult to understand why disease persists when God has so often revealed cures for various diseases, and helped us to eradicate some of them entirely. Nature has a remarkable capacity for inventing new agents of disease, or new mutations of old enemies. Almost as soon as human intelligence, ingenuity and enterprise have eliminated one viral disease (such as smallpox), another deadly virus, the one that causes AIDS, appears. Germs of all kinds flourish at the expense of their hosts and they too can develop remarkable resistance to drugs.

If I cannot plumb the depths of the mystery of disease and suffering, I can at least take a positive attitude when I encounter them. God is always with us in our sufferings and can use disease as a stepping stone towards our eventual fulfilment. God always wants us to be healed even if we cannot be cured. I shall be saying more about God and healing in a later chapter. Before that I want to discuss the recovery of a sense of being blessed, a sense that has been present in all religious traditions throughout history.

In 1983 Matthew Fox, an American scholar and Dominican friar, published a book called *Original Blessing*, in which he drew together many insights from a large number of mystical writers who wrote positively about the blessings of creation.[11] The book was greeted with enthusiasm by many thoughtful people who were dissatisfied with existing theologies. These people had been looking for more positive ways of thinking about issues of ecology, justice and peace, and they were eager to develop an appropriate spirituality for the twentieth century.

There is a proper critical method to be applied to any book, including this one, where the author selects material 'to make a point'. Fox sometimes does this with the mystical writings he uses, but his work is a good antidote to negative thinking and is welcome on that account. It has done much to offset some of the harsher aspects of the doctrine of original sin. Nevertheless, there is truth in both ways of thinking about the existence of evil. We need to hold original sin and original blessing together in our minds when we consider disease and healing.

Disease in Its Particular Forms

In its more specific sense, disease is any condition of a living creature, or some part of its body, in which functions are disturbed. We may sometimes feel 'out of sorts' or mildly unwell, but we don't usually think of ourselves as diseased until some part of our bodies cannot function in its customary way.

As Dr Osler implied, there are many complex diseases at work in creation. Many of these are caused by natural agents, such as germs and viruses, which attack host plants, animals and human beings from outside. We know that there is a delicate balance between the invasive germ or virus and the potential victim. But the same is true of diseases that arise within an organism, where one organ starts to malfunction, or a group of cells suddenly starts to multiply and form themselves into a cancer. Disease occurs when an organism or person's balance is seriously upset by some alteration in the external or internal environment.

This disturbance of balance can be brought about by an overwhelming infection, or by an external wound or burn, but it can also be triggered by mental, emotional or spiritual distress. It is no accident that someone who is very tired, or severely stressed, or is in a situation of spiritual conflict, is more prone to illness than their neighbour who is full of energy and happiness.

In 1967 an American psychiatrist, Dr Rahe, and a United States Navy doctor, Dr Arthur, showed quite conclusively that men who suffered from stress due to major lifestyle changes – such as bereavement, or divorce, or moving house or employment – were more likely to fall ill in the year after the stress.[12] Dr Rahe and Dr Arthur, and some of their other American colleagues, like Dr Harold Wolff and Dr T.H. Holmes of Cornell Medical Center, have since repeated this research, and it has been conclusively shown that there is a direct correlation between an event like bereavement (the highest scoring stress factor in the remaining spouse's life), and subsequent illness. Moreover, the higher the stress factor, the more likely it is that the subsequent illness will be a severe one.

Rahe and Arthur's important work was well documented, and was publicised by many writers at that time; in particular by Alvin Toffler who included these and other research findings in his book, *Future Shock*, published in 1972.[13] Toffler and others were concerned about the effects of rapid changes in lifestyle on individuals whose lives were increasingly affected by complex technological revolutions. Their writings helped to change people's attitudes towards stress and its effects. They also popularised some ways of counteracting strees, such as transcendental meditation, yoga and deep relaxation.

The Effects of Changes in Attitudes to Disease

The link between stress and physical disease is now generally accepted, and this has had an important effect on the way medicine has been practised over the last twenty years. These days many doctors try to look after the whole person, taking note of their patients' relationships and social environment as well as the state of their organs. This increased understanding of the connection between stress and physical disease has also had an important effect on many people's attitudes towards health and healing. In Britain, for instance, far more people now welcome holistic, or whole person, medicine. When patients feel that they are not being treated in a holistic way, they are more willing to desert orthodox, or allopathic, medical care, and to turn instead to alternative therapists.

Orthodox medical practitioners and scientists have undoubtedly reacted with some suspicion to the general public's great interest in therapies which do not rely on technological or invasive techniques. During his presidency of the British Medical Association HRH Prince Charles did much to support doctors who were interested in holistic medicine. His valedictory address in 1983 was a catalyst for a number of important initiatives, and some of the more traditional therapies that had hitherto been neglected by Western scientists are now being studied in depth and more sympathetically.[14]

Since whole person medicine is the only kind I believe in, I do not find it very useful to distinguish between physical, mental and spiritual diseases. If one does so, there is a danger of reverting to a mind-set that treats symptoms or organs and forgets the whole person. The whole of ourselves is affected by any breakdown in our ability to function. It is, for instance, comparatively simple to take out an inflamed appendix, but such an operation, even if it only means two weeks off work, may have profound effects on a financially stressed parent. A young person who suddenly gets appendicitis may find themselves unable to sit an entrance examination for university. Their morale may plummet and consequently it will take them much longer to recover.

Having said that, I must tell a story against myself to stress the need for moderation and common sense in all things. I recall with some embarrassment the day on which one of my own daughters told me she had a stomachache. She was having a bit of trouble at school at the time so I was inclined to put it down to nerves. Being in a hurry to get to work myself, I sent her upstairs to get ready for school. I waited at the bottom of the stairs for her, and as she came down I noticed that she was limping badly. Mercifully, my doctor's instincts took over. I could recognise an important and meaningful sign when I saw one. I laid her on our couch downstairs and within minutes delivered her to the casualty department of our nearby local hospital. She had acute appendicitis and it was on the point of perforating! She was limping badly because the lining of the abdomen was affected by the grossly inflamed and swollen appendix. So there are times when it is necessary to treat an organ and not a whole person!

By and large, however, I think people need to be seen in relation to all their circumstances and not just some of them. Holistic medicine takes the whole of a person into consideration whenever any symptom of disease presents itself. But it is not always enough just to think about the individual. A patient's relationships at home, at work and in the community also need looking at. It is not always the person who presents with the problem who is the cause of that breakdown in health. Often the disease is in someone else or in society as a whole.

Am I then saying that everyone who falls ill with a common cold, or appendicitis, needs to have their psychological health examined or their spiritual state probed? Or that everyone who is mildly depressed has to start investigating its causes in his or her family or community? No, of course I am not saying either of those things. Nature itself has a remarkable way of putting us right. All we need is a generous measure of common sense, good diagnosis and some tender loving care. What I am saying is that if we don't recover from an illness in a reasonable length of time, or seem to be getting worse, we need to look at the whole of our lives, and we need to find people in the healing professions and ministries who will help us do so.

The Blessings of Some Handicaps

I have left to the last the question of whether we ought to think of congenital malformations and handicaps as diseases. When the rhythms of nature are disturbed or interfered with, certain babies do not develop to their full potential. Yet, if they are born alive and survive infancy, because their physiological organs are all functioning perfectly well, they are unique people, created in the image of God. They do have potential and God is there to help them fulfil it, with our help. They offer the community into which they are born a challenge, the challenge of diversity of person and of need. Perhaps communities cannot be whole without them?

I believe it is right to ask God to heal people from their diseases. I believe that God always answers that prayer, though not always in ways that please us. I do not feel so sure about asking God to change children who are congenitally handicapped. God works mighty wonders through mentally and physically handicapped people, even those who are unhappy and disturbed. Maybe we should simply thank God for them and kneel to receive God's blessing and theirs?

31

That may seem a very hard thing to say to a family which is struggling to get the right kind of help, treatment and education for their handicapped son or daughter, but many parents would agree with me that their lives have been enriched by the joys and sufferings of living with someone who has learning difficulties and major physical handicaps.[15] Having said that, I know there are precedents for believing that God can cure anyone of any condition. After all, did Jesus not heal a man who was 'blind from birth'? He did. But should we ask him to cure a source of blessing to us? I think we sometimes should, but I am not sure we always should; whereas I am quite sure we can always ask for God's healing for everyone. So let me look at what I mean by that word.

HEALING

> I bandage; God heals.
> *Ambroise Paré (1510–1590)*[16]

Dr Ambroise Paré was a French army surgeon. He was a pioneer. Instead of cauterising amputated limb stumps with boiling oil he used ligatures to tie off the bleeding arteries and bandaged the open wounds. His famous saying points to a truth which is central to my life for I firmly believe that God is the agent of all cures, of all healings, of all our quests for wholeness. All we can do is assist in God's work.

'Healing is a very much misunderstood word,' wrote Monsignor Michael Buckley, a Roman Catholic priest who has been involved in healing for many years, in his book, *His Healing Touch*.[17] This potential for misunderstanding is largely due to the fact that we use the word healing in so many different ways. Unless we are very careful it is easy to think we are using a particular word in one way when our audience thinks we are using it in a different sense. Hence there are many opportunities for confusion. I will do my best to say what I mean as clearly as possible.

Understanding the Meaning of Healing

Healing is dynamic; it involves a change from one state of being to another. There is always some movement about it. Moreover, I believe it is something that happens all the time on our journey towards wholeness. There is a sense in which birth, growth, maturity, aging and death are all part of that natural journey. Thinking of healing in this way helps a great deal because it enables us to see the whole of life as a unity: we can understand and accept that healing is taking place all the time, even during illness and terrible suffering.

Whenever I think about it rationally I am able to see healing in this way. Often, however, I can't, because my own and other people's need for functional health over-ride my desire for wholeness. What I find I want when I am ill, or am attending others who are ill, is a cure.

Curative Healing

It is my belief that all of us will eventually become whole people. I make that statement as a Christian. This means that I want God to help me to change so that I grow more like, and closer to, God. Although I expect to die before I reach that goal, I also hope and expect that God who is Love will gather me into that Love at my life's end.

While I am alive, however, I admit that I also want to be able to function as a well person for as much of my life as possible. Whenever I am ill I want to be cured, to go back to how I felt before I was ill. In that sense, healing reverses the process that made me sick and takes me back to functional health. Yet, as we all know, health is a relative state. Even when I'm well I do not stay still. I am always travelling forward to the next moment of time, always changing, always moving towards death and my ultimate destiny. In that sense I need healing in order to move towards fulfilment and completion.

It is this backwards and forwards aspect of healing that can sometimes be quite confusing, because when people speak of healing they don't always specify exactly what it is they are

33

asking for. 'I want to be healed,' they say. Or, 'Will you pray to God to heal me?'

'Yes,' I reply, 'but what are you asking for? Do you want to go backwards, or forwards?'

When they have recovered from their astonishment that I should ask such peculiar questions, we try to sort out what they want. Are they asking to be restored to what they were before they were ill, or to go forward to become a new person, a person who is closer to wholeness than before they needed to be healed? Sometimes they are delighted to find that you can ask for both with a good conscience! But a great many people only want a cure. If their health is restored to them that is enough. They are quite content to stop there. They don't see any need to change.

Personally, I do feel a need for wholeness, but I also know that God waits patiently for us to see that need. It is no use pushing people when they are not ready to receive what God is holding out to them. It is important to leave the timing to God and the person concerned.

If people come to me asking for healing I try to discern what kind of healing they feel they need. That helps me to keep their particular need uppermost in my mind as we look together to see what can be done to help them. In my work as a doctor I have chosen to link the kind of healing that reverses illness with the idea embodied in the word cure. I have also chosen to link the healing that implies movement towards a new state of being with the word wholeness. These two kinds of healing do not contradict or cancel each other out. They are complementary. I have only separated them here for the sake of clarity.

Healing as a Movement Towards Wholeness

Healers come in all shapes and sizes. They use many different ways of healing (some of which we shall look at later on) and belong to different religious traditions, or to none at all. Does it matter? Isn't it all God's work? Well, yes, it is all God's work, whether or not it is seen as such.

I find that I have a deep affinity with all persons of faith who recognise God at work, but I also have to admit that I feel most comfortable with the Christian healing ministry, partly because I am very much at home with its language and rituals. It is also because I am convinced that Christianity roots its healing ministry in the good soil of the Church as a community of ordinary people who come together to do things with God's help that they could not do in their own strength.

Changing Attitudes Towards Healing

During the span of my working life there has undoubtedly been a shift in attitudes towards healing. When I was studying medicine forty-five years ago we thought only in terms of cure. Anything else, including death, was a failure. Now most doctors, and nearly all non-medical healers, talk about becoming whole; although, happily, they still want people to be cured as well. This change of approach has taken place slowly and patchily in my own life, but it has taken place.

When I was a young doctor I remember reading some words by Evelyn Underhill, a noted spiritual director.[18] She had died when I was a schoolgirl and I had discovered her writings when I first became a Christian. I copied these sentences down because at the time I thought they epitomised what I meant by healing. I have not been able to trace their exact origin, but I recently came across them in a book of quotations and they brought home to me how much I had changed since I first read them. These are the words:

All disease of soul or body is a subtraction from human nature, a way of being sub-standard. There are no colds in Paradise. So, healing of any sort is a kind of creative or rather regenerating work, a direct expression and furthering of God's will. It means bringing life back to what it ought to be, mending that which has broken down, healing our deep mental and spiritual wounds by the action of Christ's charity, giving new strength to the weak, new purity to the tainted.[19]

35

I agree entirely with Underhill's statement as far as it goes. It describes the kind of healing that reverses illness and brings about cures. There is nothing wrong at all in asking for that sort of healing, knowing as I do how good it is to feel well and to be able to function properly. Indeed, even today I often pray for someone to be cured (that is, restored to functional health). But it doesn't go far enough. Today I would want to add that while we cannot always be cured, we can always be healed and thus move a little closer towards wholeness.

I had to learn this distinction in quite a painful way. As a young doctor I was appointed as house physician to a children's ward. One of my patients was a delightful twelve-year-old girl who was dying from a malignant tumour. Her parents were naturally very distressed when we told them that the tumour was inoperable and that their daughter was now so ill that she was not expected to live more than a few days. They asked whether they could bring a healer to her bedside and the consultant readily gave permission.

The healer came. He seemed a very kind person. He prayed for the child. He laid his hands on her. He told the parents that she would be cured. He went away. The child grew worse. The parents became distraught. They sent for the healer again. He came. This time I stayed too because I wanted to pray with them. I heard the healer telling the parents that if they had enough faith their daughter would be cured. I felt very unhappy about what he was saying, but at the time I couldn't put my finger on what was wrong.

That night the child died. The parents felt that they had lacked the faith that would have saved her. It was terrible to see them laying the blame for her death at their own door. I, for my part, felt very angry with the healer for burdening them with such a legacy of guilt. I was too inexperienced to find any suitable words for those parents. I did what I could, and little enough it was. They left the ward and I never saw them again.

For several years after that I avoided healers and the Christian healing ministry as a whole. I continued to pray for my patients, but I never knew what to pray for. Then one day, quite by chance, I met a priest called Harry Potts who was chaplain at Burrswood, Dorothy Kerin's Home of Healing in Kent. Harry was a genial, generous, loving man. He was also a man you could talk to about anything. I did. I talked about my anger about the child who had died a long time ago. To my relief he understood, but he also told me the truth. 'God always heals,' he said, 'but in his way, not ours.'

Healing as a Whole Ministry

Harry and others gradually taught me to pray for healing and to leave the way it would happen to God. It might include a cure. It might include suffering. It might include recovery to full function, but it might also include having to come to terms with partial or complete disability. It might include death. It would never include blaming parents or relatives, leaving someone without hope, or castigating anyone for his or her unhealthy ways of life, faults or sins. It would always include treating someone with faith and hope and above all love.

So the Christian healing ministry became part of my own life and I have never ceased to thank God for allowing me to become part of that ministry as well as a doctor. It was not that I stopped being a doctor, or stopped using all the scientific means at my disposal in the service of patients who came to me for advice and help. It simply meant that I could add to that service the ministries of prayer and the laying on of hands. If my patients were Christians, and wanted it, I also sometimes put them in touch with the sacramental ministries which the Church offers to all her members.

I have taken part in the Christian healing ministry for many years. I have come to appreciate the enormous diversity of ways in which God can heal, and the rich variety of people who are used in this ministry. I have learnt to work with all kinds of people. Above all I have learnt that under God the principal agent of healing is the patient who seeks health.

Healing Relationships

As I have gained experience, so too my ideas about healing have expanded. There was a time when I only thought of healing in relation to an individual who was sick. Gradually I came to see that healing was also appropriate for people who had problems with personal relationships (including those with God), for groups of people in trouble and for whole communities at war with each other. Of course I myself am involved with only a tiny handful of people, but at least I can contribute in a small way to God's continuous healing work in the world.

God always does what is best for us. We may be cured instantly, we may not be restored to functional health at all, but we will always be healed. As I have grown older I have become more patient. I have ceased to want instant cures, although I am always glad when they happen. I have learnt to be pleased with partial cures, or with gradual healing, or with one tiny step towards wholeness. God works in mysterious ways, often over prolonged periods of time, and I am content to wait on his time and to help others to do so too.

Sharing the Healing

Before I end this section on the meaning of healing and begin to look at more specific and practical ways in which we human beings can take part in God's healing work, I want to look at the way in which a healed person shares his or her healing with others. Whenever I have met a person who has been healed, or who is very close to being a whole person, I have been deeply impressed by the way in which she or he shares that healing. So I want to tell the story of a man whom I have only met through the pages of a book.[20] His name is Dr Nagai. He was an eminent Japanese radio-therapist who was also a Christian.

On 9 August 1945, at 11 am, the second atom bomb, 'Fat Man', plummeted down from a B-29 bomber on to Nagasaki. Dr Nagai, already a sick man, was working in the hospital at the time. He was blown across the room by the blast and temporarily trapped under a pile of debris and glass. When he was freed by some of his staff he and they began to search for survivors. Later they were to learn that 80 per cent of the hospital patients and staff had died. Despite his wounds, and despite his intense desire to look for his own wife, Dr Nagai's courage that day raised the morale of his surviving colleagues. Together they went about their ghastly task of uncovering the burnt remains of their colleagues. Together they tried to ease the suffering of those who were dying of horrible wounds and extensive radiation burns.

Two days later, an exhausted Dr Nagai went home. There he found the charred remains of his wife, Midori. All that was left of her was her skull, her pelvic bones and her spinal column. By these burnt fragments of the woman he loved, he found her cherished rosary, almost entirely melted. As he stood there, something extraordinary happened. Instead of cursing God and the Americans who had obliterated his wife and thousands of other people, Dr Nagai found himself blessing God and giving thanks. Later he wrote a book about his experience.

Dr Nagai's writings are full of serenity, acceptance and forgiveness. It seems that almost immediately after he had buried his wife, he started to walk to Koba where he had left his two children and their grandmother for safety. On the way a verse from the New Testament took hold of him: 'the heavens and the earth will pass away but my words will never pass away.' (Luke 21:33). His biographer tells us:

> He repeated the verse again and again, in rhythm with his walking . . . He felt his new mantra flood his body, soul and spirit, and with it came a consciousness that everything was alright. Midori had merely finished her work early and gone home to God.[21]

Dr Nagai knew that he too would die without seeing his two children grow to maturity. He was already suffering from leukaemia, due to radiation from the early X-ray machines whose use he had pioneered in Japan. Three months later he developed severe symptoms of atomic bomb radiation sickness. Prayers were made to Maximillian Kolbe, a Polish priest who had died heroically in Auschwitz concentration camp in August 1941, and to Christ.

Dr Nagai recovered sufficiently to return to work for a time. He began to write, and to preach about sacrificial love. He saw the bombing of his beloved city of Nagasaki in the context of his belief that Nagasaki was *hansai*, a whole burnt offering, an atoning sacrifice which brought about peace.[22] On 23 November 1945 he ended the sermon he preached at a requiem mass for Nagasaki's dead with the words:

> The Lord has given. The Lord has taken away. Blessed be the name of the Lord. Let us be thankful that Nagasaki was chosen for the whole-burnt sacrifice! Let us be thankful that through this sacrifice peace was granted to the world and religious freedom to Japan.[23]

These words and Dr Nagai's subsequent writings on the same theme had a profound effect on Christians and non-Christians in his country. Not everybody agreed with him, but they listened. From that time on Dr Nagai wrote, and wrote, and wrote. His first book, *The Bells of Nagasaki*, was completed on the anniversary of Midori's death. By that time he was seriously ill again. He never worked as a doctor or left his bed until his death five years later on the first day of May, 1951. He was forty-three years old.

During those five years in bed, Dr Nagai used every scrap of energy he had to promote the gospel of love. He was, you might say, consumed with love, for his children, for those who visited him, for lepers to whom he wrote faithfully, for his countrymen and women, for his Emperor who came to see him during a pilgrimage to Nagasaki in May, 1949.

Everyone who met him, or received a letter from him, felt better for the contact. A blind leper testified how he had been saved from despair and suicide by Nagai's letters:

> I despaired and attempted suicide. Yet here was Nagai who had lost everything, was dying, and was at peace with himself and

the world. The matron kept reading us Nagai and he began writing to us. He led me to Christ and the Faith that discovers everything in life is a gift and a grace. It is fifty years since I became a leper and I can say: 'Thank God for my leprosy and thank God for Nagai.'[24]

Truly this man radiates joy and peace in the midst of suffering. His gospel is simple, yet profound: thank God for everything, including suffering; allow love to transform your suffering; glorify God by your living and your dying.

It so happened that I was ill myself when I first read about Dr Nagai. His witness protected me from self-pity and encouraged me by example. But he did more than that. He made me feel better. The wounded healer, the whole man that he had become, came to meet me in my woundedness, and we met in Christ. That is what healing is all about.

CHAPTER THREE

In Tune with Nature

From Harmony, from heavenly Harmony
This universal Frame began:
From Harmony to Harmony
Through all the Compass of the Notes it ran
The diapason closing full in Man.

John Dryden (1631–1700)[1]

NATURE'S HEALING RHYTHMS

Dryden's poem, written in 1687 in honour of St Cecilia, patron saint of music, used the image of musical harmony to describe the very nature of God, the three persons of the Trinity co-existing and co-creating in perfect harmony. It is an apt analogy, for God creates the universe in accordance with natural laws, themselves created by God, just as musical composers have to be aware of the mathematical laws of harmony, even if they also break those laws from time to time to incorporate discord into a composition.

In the seventeenth century, when Dryden was writing his poetry, the virtues of harmonious music and melodious poetry were much extolled, but nowadays we can also appreciate the inclusion of disharmonies and discords. If wisely handled, these can contribute positively to music and the spoken word. There is a sense in which our twentieth-century eyes and ears are well attuned to discord; providing that it is kept in proportion it can add piquancy and even beauty to the whole composition.

One of the most exciting changes during this century has been our acceptance that discord can be a positive quality. Its very presence highlights the absence of harmony, evoking a desire in the beholder, or listener, to reconcile all the different elements in the work of art. Nowhere is this truer than in creation itself. Our understanding of the created world has taken a leap forward during this century, largely through the insights of physicists into the structure of matter.

The possible relation between healing and the physical composition of matter involves some quite complex discussion of the work of certain modern physicists. You may like to skip the theoretical bits, but before you do so I'd like to explain why I think it is so important for readers to struggle with them. This is because healing is an area of human experience which is subject to many conflicting opinions. Some scientists would like to discount all healings that cannot be substantiated by hard evidence of a change in tissues which had previously been conclusively shown to be diseased. If they can't explain it, they won't accept that healing has really occurred. Some doctors who take this view would pour scorn on anyone who said that a 'spiritual' activity like meditation or prayer could produce structural changes in the body.

On the other hand, some religious people would wish to claim many healings as miracles, despite any lack of firm evidence. Some of them would go so far as to claim, for instance, that if a medically treated cancer disappeared in a person who had been prayed for, then that cure was entirely the result of prayer, or divine intervention, rather than the scientific treatment, despite the well-known fact that cancer can be cured by scientific treatment.

Such conflicting views, which I have admittedly expressed as extremes, prevent us understanding the miracle of natural healing, by which I mean creation's tendency to heal itself spontaneously. If we could understand how nature works towards healing we might be in a better position to understand why, for instance, meditation can produce measurable changes in the body and why some cancers do seem to regress more quickly when prayer is offered and others disappear altogether, against all expectations, when no prayer has apparently been made.

In my early days as a qualified doctor, before I had become

involved in the Christian healing ministry, a man came to see me after he had been diagnosed as having a rapidly growing cancerous tumour in his lung. A biopsy had been taken. The radiographic diagnosis had been confirmed. As was the custom at the time, the hospital doctors had not told this man of his diagnosis. As far as he was concerned he had a nasty cough due to some inflammation that the doctors had said 'would take a long time to settle down.'

When I saw this patient I too decided to keep quiet about his condition, though I told his wife that he had an inoperable cancer. She and I waited for the rogue cells to overwhelm the healthy tissues and eventually kill her husband. He did not die. Instead he recovered. Years and years later he died of a sudden heart attack. At a post mortem the lungs were inspected. The site of the cancer was just a tiny localised shrivelled-up fibrous nodule. Something in that disordered unstable system had brought order out of chaos. The balance between the host and his disease was restored, the cancer was held in check and the man was spontaneously healed. We did not know how it had happened, or why it had happened in this man and not in others.

For many years I remembered this man, without having any theory about what had happened to cure him of his cancer. It is only recently that scientists and people who use prayer and meditation for healing have begun to work together to think about why healing occurs. The breakthrough has come about largely through the work of some physicists who have taken an interest in Eastern techniques of meditation.

This is why I have to ask you to ask you to struggle with some of the ideas propounded by modern physicists whose investigations into the structure of matter give us some hint of patterns of behaviour in creation which might encourage tissue healing.

Physicists like Ernest Rutherford,[2] Albert Einstein[3] and Niels Bohr[4] have done us all a service by explaining their findings in ways that can be understood by non-physicists. One of their successors, Fritjof Capra,[5] a research physicist, has drawn attention to some qualities that are inherent in creation. Three insights stand out in relation to healing: the first is that matter and energy are interconnected;[6] the second, that polarity, the holding together of opposites, is inherent in all nature;[7] the third is that there is 'a continual cosmic dance of energy' in the universe. That is to say that matter is intrinsically dynamic, the whole universe being 'engaged in endless motion and activity.'[8]

The Interconnectedness of Matter and Energy

It is virtually impossible to give a condensed explanation of the quantum physics outlined in Capra's book.[9] Essentially he expounds the way in which Newton's mechanical model of the universe has been replaced by the discoveries of modern physics. The following quotation gives a hint of the revolution in thinking that he describes:

> Quantum theory has demolished the classical concepts of solid objects and of strictly deterministic laws of nature. At the sub-atomic level, the solid material objects of classical physics dissolved into wave-like patterns of probabilities and these patterns, ultimately, do not represent probabilities of things, but rather probabilities of interconnections . . . As we penetrate into matter, nature does not show us any isolated 'basic building blocks', but rather appears as a complicated web of relations between the various parts of the whole.[10]

This idea that matter can behave like waves, that matter and energy are intimately interconnected in a complicated web of relations, leads on to the proposition that energy can be generated and released in ways that both spring from matter and affect matter. In a later passage Capra says that: All particles can be transmuted into other particles; they can be created from energy and can vanish into energy.[11]

I don't think it is at all easy to grasp the quantum theory of physics and I don't pretend to understand it in detail.[12] However, despite the fact that theories about sub-atomic physics are continually changing and developing, I find that they do help me to understand something about the patterns and relationships that exist in nature.

Capra's exegesis – together with the writings of Dr John Polkinghorne, a mathematical physicist and theologian,[13] who disagrees with Capra on a number of issues, and who relates quantum physics to Christian theology – have encouraged me to think about how energy within nature is released in healing.

Although I don't want to apply the observations and interpretations of sub-atomic physics directly to medicine, I do think one can speak by analogy. In that sense, I can begin to understand how 'spiritual' activities like meditation and prayer can affect matter. The willingness of Zen and transcendental meditators to subject themselves to scientific examination has enabled scientists to document some of the physical effects of meditation.[14] Moreover, doctors – like Dr Deepak Chopra, who was trained in Western-style medicine before studying Ayurvedic medicine, and who is a transcendental meditator – are now exploring the relationship between mind-body and quantum physics.[15] The insights of scientists who have studied ancient forms of healing, such as Ayurvedic medicine and transcendental meditation (which I shall be looking at again in Chapter Six), need to be taken seriously by Western scientists so that we can all begin to understand how natural healing takes place. When we have explored this a bit further we might be able to find better ways of promoting healing.

Polarity in Nature

The second insight of modern physicists is about the creative tension between opposites that exists in nature. The ancient Chinese sages spoke of the archetypal poles of yin and yang. They suggested that there was a creative tension between them and that the dynamic interplay between opposites was present in all natural phenomena and in all human situations. Quite early in this century Niels Bohr suggested that these beliefs would be helpful to us in considering the nature of matter.[16]

The classical physicists believed that matter consisted of atoms, that were in turn composed of particles, which were the indestructible units of matter. Bohr and the quantum physicists, however, said that electrons behaved both like waves and like particles. They considered that these descriptions in terms of particles and waves were complementary, interconnected and inter-dependent.

In the sub-atomic world, matter and energy are interchangeable, but certain characteristics (quantum numbers) must persist. Matter and anti-matter can exist in symmetry, and, in certain circumstances, the interaction between particles and anti-particles can lead to the annihilation of both, with an immense release of energy in the process.[17] The principle of polarity is very widespread in nature. Light and dark, life and death, are seen as opposites but they are in fact interdependent and they manifest their interplay in the struggle to maintain a proper balance. These are polarities of concept, rather than the kind of physical polarities we find in the subatomic world, but they nevertheless point to the truth that nature contains within itself the means of holding extremes in balance, and this has implications for the healing disciplines.

Polarity has been extended to include many concepts, some of which are irrelevant to our consideration of healing. Others, like the idea that the existence of evil is essential to bring out the good in created beings, are relevant but not at this point. What we need to think about now is the way in which creative tensions between opposites within a person can work to their benefit when they are struggling to find a balance within themselves and their internal and external environment. If, for instance, a group of cancerous cells suddenly starts to multiply, thereby upsetting the balance between healthy host tissues and aberrant rogue cells, is there a way to restore that balance without cutting out the abnormal tissue or destroying it with radiotherapy or chemotherapy? Can the two types of cells be maintained in a proper polarity with each other?

There are many healers (Ayurvedic and others) who would say that the body itself can release energy that will restore the balance and contain the cancer, or even effect its regression. They often use mental energy to localise and isolate the cancerous tissue.[18] At present I do not think there is enough scientific evidence to show whether or not such 'balancing acts' work, but I certainly think that nature has its own way of maintaining the balance between healthy tissue and rogue cells. Much more work needs to be done on this mysterious interplay between a victim and his or her disease.

Modern physicists have helped to give us an understanding of how polarity works in nature, particularly concerning the interconnections of chaos and order, and of chance and necessity. John Polkinghorne's book *Science and Creation* takes his readers deep into these matters. His work leads to a greater understanding of how natural movement towards wholeness can occur, even when chaos appears to rule, and when logical probability seems to exclude the possibility of chance producing wholeness. In an important chapter on the interconnectedness of order and disorder, Polkinghorne comments:

> While the second law of thermodynamics proclaims that change and decay in all around we see, we are also aware of systems which seem to be swimming against the tide of increasing entropy. They develop and maintain an order, in contrast to the increasing disorder around them. We ourselves are examples of such systems, as we maintain in being the intricate patterns of our bodies. The fact is that in appropriate circumstances the instabilities of dynamical systems can actually prove to be the triggers of order rather than chaos.[19]

Statements like that help me to understand the mysterious events that occur in some people who recover unexpectedly from illness, like the patient I spoke of who recovered from lung cancer. I think that his recovery had something to do with this interconnectedness between order and chaos.

Polarity is perhaps easier to understand when we are not thinking about particles and waves or normal and abnormal cells. There are many opposites which co-exist in our own personalities, and we may sometimes become aware of a major and exhausting internal conflict. This can be so severe that we become ill. Healing, in such instances, means restoring the balance so that the polar opposites can be integrated into a healthy unity.

A good example of this can be seen in a husband and wife who are having moderately severe marital problems. When everything is relatively all right there is a healthy balance between feelings of love and feelings of hate. Every husband, for instance, will experience moments of hatred when his wife does something that intensely irritates him; and the converse is true. Suppose that one day the wife goes too far. The husband's internal balance gets upset and he begins to feel hatred more often and more deeply than before. He begins to notice all kinds of things about his wife that he never noticed when they were first married. He forgets the love that is still there in the background and begins to find fault with his wife all the time. If this continues over a long period, sooner or later separation or divorce becomes inevitable.

An external friend or counsellor coming into such a situation would know that where there is hatred there is also love. If two people are totally indifferent to each other there is probably nothing left alive in the marriage, but the presence of one strong emotion probably indicates the presence of its counterpart. The outsider's task would be to reawaken that love so that the balance of nature could be restored and the whole relationship could be seen in its true perspective. That cannot be done by exhortation. It can only be done by a patient uncovering of what is already there. Ideally the outsider would provide a calm, secure atmosphere that allowed the husband and wife to make that discovery for themselves rather than being told about it.

Much the same is true of the balance between good and evil in every individual. Spiritual sickness is often very distressing to a person who is longing to be united with God, yet who is also painfully aware of the reality of personal sin. The struggle to cleave to God sets up a pull in the opposite direction which can be so strong that one feels totally 'possessed' by evil. This conflict can be very powerful and can cause distress.

Sometimes victims who feel that they are being taken over by evil, which they cannot bear to acknowledge as their own, will project their condition on to an external enemy such as the devil. In fact they are not 'possessed' by outside forces at all but are captive to their own destructive emotions. In such a case, a healer needs to help the individual experience the polarity of good and evil within themselves. In saying this I am not denying the reality of the devil. True demonic possession can occur, but it is very rare. This kind of self-generated conflict is much more common. The cure for such a spiritual sickness, whether it emanates from the person or from a spiritual enemy called the devil, is similar. In both cases the victim has to integrate their personality in such a way that good and evil can co-exist in balance with each other, with the bias being towards goodness.

The Cosmic Dance of Energy in Nature

The third of Capra's insights that I feel to be important in healing is that there is a 'continual cosmic dance of energy in nature'.[20] This dance has to do with the rhythms that are inherent in matter, with particles and anti-particles, with nuclei and electrons, with what Capra refers to as 'an energy dance; a pulsating process of creation and destruction.'[21] John Polkinghorne sees the dance of creation in a somewhat different way. He says: 'The metaphor of the dance of creation succeeds in holding together the ideas of ordered pattern and flexible movement in a way that is congenial to the sort of idea I am trying to pursue.'[22] Polkinghorne applies that idea to the workings of the unconscious mind. To me, the pattern of order and flexibility finds its fullest expression in the rhythms of the brain.

We now know a great deal about the electro-chemical processes in the brain. We can also observe wave patterns in the brain by using electro-encephalography (EEG) to measure the various voltage fluctuations and rhythms produced under different conditions. A soundly sleeping brain, for instance, produces what is called a delta rhythm, that is voltages that peak between one and four times a second. A dreaming or drowsy brain produces voltages that reach their maximal state four to seven times per second. These are called theta waves. When people are awake and alert but very relaxed they produce alpha waves which oscillate between eight and thirteen times a second. Once they begin to think and move, things speed up and the voltages peak in the range of thirteen to thirty cycles a second. This is known as the beta rhythm. Under certain circumstances human beings can become aware of their various brain rhythms, so much so that they can control their rate through concentration.

In the 1970s there was a lot of scientific research into sleep and relaxation rhythms in the brain and people were trained to produce alpha waves by using bio-feedback machines for relaxation. The machine I tried out at that time was very simple. It depended on the measurement of skin resistance. I put a finger cuff on to my left forefinger and another on to my right forefinger. Both were attached by a lead to a little black box which emitted a beep when I had relaxed enough to alter the skin resistance. When I first started using it I had to wait quite a while before I reached that state of tranquillity, but I soon learnt. I subsequently tested myself out with an EEG and my feeling of deep relaxation was associated with an increase in my EEG alpha waves. I can now reach that state of peacefulness quite easily without any equipment.

It has been shown that alpha waves are beneficial to the whole human body. As Lyall Watson, a biologist, has said:

> Deep relaxation, whether it is induced by alphameters or by easily mastered techniques such as transcendental meditation, is a state with clealy defined physiological correlates. Anyone in this condition shows, in addition to slow alpha and theta waves – a decrease in oxygen consumption; a reduction in carbon dioxide elimination; reductions in heart rate, blood pressure, blood lactate, blood cortisone and muscle tone; and increases in finger temperature, the perfusion [i.e. reduction in circulation] of internal organs and basal skin resistance . . . [23]

This state of relaxation is often known as the fourth state of consciousness, to distinguish it from wakefulness, light (or rapid eye movement) sleep and deep sleep. It certainly seems to be beneficial. People who practise Zen or transcendental meditation, or who learn to relax with bio-feedback machines, feel better and more energetic, and become less anxious and tense. Some claim to have a heightened awareness of reality and of the network of relationships between themselves and all created beings. Their descriptions of their experiences are similar to those of mystics.

Bio-feedback has caught on. It is sometimes used by doctors and other professionals in the treatment of stress-related conditions. It can also be used to control particular kinds of epilepsy, because the alpha waves sometimes over-ride the irregular patterns of the brain which can cause epileptic fits. There are hundreds of thousands of meditators all over the world who enjoy their daily sessions of relaxation.

I have perhaps stretched the concept of 'the continual cosmic dance of energy' a bit far in applying it to the dancing rhythms of the brain, but I wonder? Surely the dance of the atoms is reflected in the dance of the brain waves. As Lyall Watson comments:

> In the new physics, nothing is impossible. Some things are less likely than others, but anything can happen. Mind and matter co-exist, the state of systems depends on those observing them, and it no longer makes sense to separate the physical world from the psychical world.[24]

I have spent a considerable amount of time discussing the discoveries of modern physics in relation to healing because I believe that one of the best ways of treating sickness is to encourage an ill person to be in tune with nature, to allow the body to put itself right, to give it the right conditions to do so. It seems to me that God works directly or indirectly through either science or prayer and meditation, or both together.

Co-operating with Nature's Innate Healing Capacity

We all know that when we catch a common cold we are likely to get well within a week, whether or not we treat ourselves with cold remedies. Nature will put us right. Similarly, if we cut ourselves, the cut will heal by itself provided it is not too extensive, or too deep, and does not get infected. Most of us go to bed for a few days, or stay off work, or struggle on and wait impatiently for the cold to pass, or the cut to heal itself. Knowing how to co-operate with nature when illnesses are more complex is, however, another matter altogether. It is then that many of us turn to allopathic medical practitioners, to alternative therapies and to natural healers for help.

As soon as we start consulting practitioners of various healing therapies we are likely to feel bewildered by the vast variety of treatments on offer. In Chapter Six I shall offer some advice on finding the right kind of help, but here I simply want to outline some guiding principles.

Let us suppose that you develop an illness like acute arthritis, a painful stiffness of one or many joints. You go to your doctor and a diagnosis is made. This is a most important part of finding out how to co-operate with nature because you need to know what it is you are confronting. Let us imagine you are told that you have a common complaint, such as early osteo-arthritis. The pain is bad at the moment so you are told to rest, or to take some pain-killers.

What is happening? The doctor knows that many people recover from an attack of arthritis quite spontaneously. All she or he is doing is allowing nature to restore you to health by resting the joint. While you are waiting you are also likely to be given some pain-killers or anti-inflammatory drugs to enable your joints to move without too much pain and to reduce the inflammation. If the pain gets worse, or settles into a chronic state, then the doctor may try other, more powerful drugs. He or she will also begin to worry about the stiffness that might lock that joint and prevent it from moving efficiently again, so a course of physiotherapy might be recommended. Only if all these measures fail will replacement surgery be advocated.

Orthodox doctors are often the best people to go to if you want to co-operate with nature, though sometimes they are too impatient and intervene too soon. At the same time, however, your anxiety about your condition and its implications for your life might cause the disease process in your joints to accelerate. What do you do then? Well, some people grumble about it, but put up with the pain. Others try copper bracelets or use a remedy suggested to them by someone else. Others will return to their doctor. Many people turn to alternative therapies for help.

If you try out alternative therapies you are rightly looking for a cure, a complete disappearance of symptoms and of the disease process itself. So you might start by consulting a herbalist, or a chiropractor, or an osteopath, or an acupuncturist or a reflexologist. It's quite hard to decide where to begin. Perhaps someone else recommends one of these practitioners. Do you just go on their advice? Maybe you do, if you trust them. Or maybe, like me, you want to know a bit more about what you are getting involved with. I went to the public library and asked for some books on alternative therapies.

I must say that I am very impressed with the quality of some of these books. None of the ones I consulted presented their particular therapies as panaceas. All of them contained sections on their limitations. Here is a doctor who is also a qualified osteopath:

> Many conditions, such as arthritis caused by infection, are unsuitable for osteopathic treatment. But when in doubt a good osteopath will always ask you to see your own doctor.[25]

And a chiropractor:

> Someone suffering from chronic arthritis throughout the body might benefit more from a system of treatment such as acupuncture than from chiropractic treatment.[26]

And an acupuncturist, referring to rheumatoid arthritis:

54

The damage that has been done to joints cannot be improved by acupuncture, yet successful relief of pain is almost always accompanied by a reduction in the swelling over the joints – provided the disease is not in an active stage.[27]

These kinds of comments give me confidence, and they should reassure anyone who is seeking help. If you took action to consult a practitioner of alternative medicine I hope you would find someone who inspired that kind of confidence and who wasn't unrealistic about what he or she could offer. I shall be discussing some of these alternative therapies in more detail in Chaper Six.

In the meantime, let us continue to use this model to find out what to do next. Let us say that you have had several sessions with your friendly neighbourhood acupuncturist. The pain improves, though you continue to feel stiff in the mornings, and you become aware that you are rather tense about your condition because you know very well that it might eventually limit your mobility, or even cripple you. Is there anything more you should do to help nature to cure you, or to limit the progress of the disease, or to make you whole despite it? Yes, I think there is. I am always in favour of treating the whole person rather than a diseased part or organ.

It would be perfectly proper in these circumstances to try to reduce external stress. Many people, for instance, would advocate certain diets as helpful to those with arthritis. An American osteopath, Giraud W. Campbell, recommends the elimination of red meat, tea, coffee, cocoa, packaged foods, sugar and alcohol from the diet. He urges sufferers from arthritis to eat plenty of fish, poultry and lamb, fresh vegetables and raw fruit. You might choose to give such a diet a trial.[28]

Alternatively, you might know that you were suffering from internal emotional stress. If that were so the stress might cause you to tighten up your muscles, thereby increasing the pain of the inflamed joint. In that case you might wish to reduce that stress by learning a relaxation technique, such as transcendental meditation which uses a silently uttered mantra (usually a meaningless syllable) to produce deep relaxation. It has to be taught by recognised teachers of whom there are many. Alternatively, you might choose to go to someone who was a trained reflexologist, skilled in foot and hand massage, to help you relax.[29]

Reflexology is not linked to any philosophy or religion and yet it can be helpful to people of all beliefs and of none. It is based on the idea that our hands and feet are linked to other areas of the body so that massaging specific areas of our extremities can show up areas of weakness and also promote relaxation and healing in parts that have been shown to be vulnerable, sensitive or lacking in some way.

Reflexology is comparatively simple to learn and easy to offer as a service. It is very soothing to have one's feet and hands massaged, it doesn't involve undressing or embarrassment about one's bodily size or appearance, nor does it require the client to be agile or capable of physical exertion! It uses touch, which is precious in a world where many people suffer from not being touched. One of its exponents and practitioners, a Dominican nun called Sister Anne Alcock, has said:

> I often find that people cry the first time they have reflexology. Many people haven't had their feet touched since they were babies and it seems to trigger an incredible emotional release inside them . . . Reflexology is about giving and receiving – to give not in the erotic sense but giving touch without the usual connotations and that can be very powerful.[30]

If, like me, you are initially rather shy about having your feet or hands touched by another person, you can explore the possibilities of reflexology with the aid of a do-it-yourself tape recording which Sister Anne uses to help people learn to touch themselves in a loving, caring and wholesome way.[31] I found the exercises easy to follow, simple to carry out and instantly beneficial in that I was able to relax very quickly and enjoyably. An added bonus for me was that Sister Anne combines her reflexology exercises with quietly contemplative guided meditations on the psalms and other scriptural passages. That would not suit everyone, but as a Christian I welcome this creative partnership between a scientific art and a creative activity like prayer or meditation.

This is one relaxation technique which may be helpful, but there are many other techniques as well. If you want to discover more about them you will need to look around a bit, especially in conjunction with alternative medical practices and Christian healing centres. Nearly all the healing centres listed on p. 153 will have access to information about different relaxation techniques.

Having tried one alternative therapy, you might graduate to aromatherapy, massage with specific healing oils, or whole body massage. Another way of reducing stress would be to seek out a good friend or a professional counsellor with whom you could have an open discussion about your fears.

Many people would stop there, but I wouldn't. As a Christian, I believe that the harm I do through sin hurts me as well as those against whom I sin. Sometimes that hurt expresses itself in physical symptoms. Whenever I'm ill I need to take my need for forgiveness and reconciliation seriously. So, quite quietly and peacefully, I look at close relationships to see if there are sins in myself that I need to bring to the surface in open repentance, so that I can know God's forgiveness and experience his healing love. There is a very ancient tradition in the Christian church which is mentioned in the letter that James wrote to some early Christians:

> Are any among you sick? They should call for the elders of the
> church and have them pray over them, anointing them with oil
> in the name of the Lord. The prayer of faith will save the sick,
> and the Lord will raise them up; and anyone who has
> committed sins will be forgiven. Therefore, confess your sins to
> one another, and pray for one another, so that you may be
> healed. The prayer of the righteous is powerful and effective.[32]

I have mentioned this tradition here, although I shall be writing about it more specifically later because this passage of scripture contains certain elements which are valuable to a wider group of people than the ones for whom it was written. They are all about being in tune with the natural harmonies that need reinforcing if we are to become whole people.

The first element is to do with prayer. When you allow someone to come close, to pray over you, you are inviting them into your life. You are admitting your helplessness. You are openly asking for their help. It is like feeling rather lonely or unhappy without knowing exactly why, and in that state going to visit someone you trust and respect. When you come close to them they seem to know, without your telling them, that there is something wrong. Perhaps they are sensitive enough to put their finger on the cause of your trouble. Perhaps they don't know, but are willing to just sit with you as you cry. They are content to do that without asking you any awkward questions, unless, of course, you find yourself telling them about your problems. That's something that has quite often happened to me: I've gone to see a friend and then found myself talking about a problem I hardly knew was there until the moment I started talking.

To invite someone else to come close is to open yourself to the healing rhythms that may be in them. There is a kind of subconscious merging of their prayer and your prayer; their beneficence and your potential goodness; their healing harmonies and yours.

If, as well as praying over you, your friends, or the wise people James called 'elders', lay their hands on you for healing, then the close contact seems to increase the exchange between you in a number of different ways.

Firstly, someone who is an agent of healing can discern through his or her hands where the problem lies and often what is causing it. The hands and the brain seem to be deeply in tune with each other in some people, and through their hands thoughts come into their minds which very often turn out to have relevance to the other person's problems.

Secondly, someone who is a sensitive channel for healing will often be able to focus energy in her or his hands. Kirlian photography is said to have shown that some people's hands emit thermal energy.[33] This energy is transmitted to the person receiving the laying on of hands. The recipient often feels a considerable amount of warmth coming to him or her, and the warmth is quite often penetrating.[34] These healing energies somehow reinforce the energies and rhythms in all of us; and the donor's energy seems to release energy within the recipient. Such healing touches are a blessing.

Thirdly, to touch someone is to enter into intimacy with them. It is to offer and receive the token of affection and love. There must be many people who feel quite isolated and yet don't feel able to enter into close relationships because they are afraid of touching or being touched. We all know how good it can be to be touched by a nurse who has been trained to use her or his hands firmly but gently in caring for patients. Calling for trusted friends or 'elders' can be a bit like that. It can set us free to experience that intimacy in a safe way. It often releases a great deal of emotion which has a cathartic and very healing effect on both patients and healers. Anyone interested in these or other aspects of touch needs to read Norman Autton's classic study, *Touch – an exploration*, published in 1989.[35]

The passage I quoted from James' letter talks about confession of sin. The relationship between sin and sickness is a difficult one to discuss. I have found that excessive guilt about quite small (or even imagined) sins can do far more harm than the wrong-doing itself. People who are too scrupulous, or who suffer from an excessive sense of unworthiness, need help to affirm their goodness rather than being allowed to reprove themselves. However, there are times when someone is conscious of having done real harm to other people. She or he may feel quite burdened because there seems to be no way of putting the wrong right. The guilt is real enough and may get in the way of that person's healing. On such occasions it may be good to share that burden of guilt with a trustworthy person. By doing so the burden is often lifted, as if the guilty person has made symbolic restitution to the one who has been wronged. I am not talking here about ritual confession to God in the presence of a priest, but about the open admission of our failures and faults to another human being. It seems that honesty between people enables the one who feels the guilt to relinquish the past and to make a fresh start. In this way that person can recover some self-esteem and confidence with which to go forward into the future.

There is nothing specifically Christian about the features I have described. They are part of all healing. They certainly occur among Christians, but they are also present in people who make no claim to be Christians, or who have no faith at all, in the power of the healer or in any other agency. We also have to remember that many people who are atheists, or agnostics, or belong to non-Christian religious traditions, are able to help sick people through their ministries of presence, closeness and consolation.

My own observations of healers from many different backgrounds, together with the experience of people who have been to healers who make no appeal to faith, convinces me that many healings are simply a consequence of 'tuning in' to natural rhythms that surround us, co-exist with us and are in us all.

The 'prayer of faith that saves the sick' is something different, and has, I believe, more to do with ultimate salvation than with the kind of health-in-life that I have been talking about. I will discuss this kind of prayer (which I do associate exclusively with Christianity) in a later chapter.

I want to turn now to people who seem more attuned to nature's rhythms than others; they are able to pick up vibrations, memory traces and intra-psychic disturbances. They can be much concerned with healing, although they can also use their gifts very destructively. Any serious consideration of healing and healers must take note of such people who are unusually aware of the attitudes, feelings and circumstances of other people. They are sometimes called 'psychic sensitives' and that is the term I have used in the next chapter.

CHAPTER FOUR

Psychic Sensitivity

Something unknown is doing we don't know what.
Sir Arthur Eddington (1882–1944)[1]

Uncovering the Unknown

In 1955 I went on pilgrimage to Assisi. I went with a friend. We travelled by car and arrived at our destination very early in the morning. It was about 5.30am. The sun was just coming up and there was a wonderful blue haze over the town as we came down a hill and on to a quiet approach road, which led to a steeper road up another hill, towards the great basilica built in St Francis' honour.

We got out of the car, intending to walk to the places we had come to see. As we crossed the road and approached the upward slope I was a little ahead of my friend. Suddenly I felt her tug my shoulder and heard her say, 'Look where you're going, Una. You're walking straight into that wall!'

I looked up. There was no wall – none that I could see anyway. I looked at my friend, wondering if she was all right. We had driven through the night, to avoid the traffic, and I knew she was pretty tired.

'There's no wall, Cecil.'

'Yes, there is,' she insisted. 'You're right by it. Put your hand out and you'll touch it.'

'Are you feeling all right?' I said.

'Of course, I am.'

I looked at her again. Her face was slightly pale and there were tiny beads of sweat on her chin. Her eyes were a little fixed and she looked as if she were staring into the middle distance. I decided to say nothing more.

'Come on, Cecil,' I said quietly. 'I'm longing to see Assisi. It

61

says in my guidebook that we can visit the Convent of San Damiano and see St Clare's tomb.'

We went on slowly up the hill. It was still very early and the streets were deserted. When we got to the huge basilica we sat down in the crypt and fell into silent prayer. Cecil seemed more like herself, though she was much quieter than usual.

I was thankful for the silence. I still felt vaguely uneasy. I wondered if Cecil was hallucinating. Was this an early sign of illness? Or had the heat affected her? My Italian wasn't very good and I wondered what I was going to do if she became really unwell.

The church began to fill with people. We stayed to hear Mass and then went out into the brilliant sunshine. It was a lovely day and we sat down to have our picnic breakfast which we had brought from the car. Cecil was looking pink again and seemed to be wide awake.

'Did something happen?' she said.

'Yes,' I replied. 'You saw a wall where there wasn't one.'

'How odd! I remember feeling as if I were a long way away from you, and you were in some kind of danger: I wanted to tell you to keep away.'

I laughed. 'Well, anyway, you're OK now. Come on, let's go and see the Convent of the Poor Clares.'

The rest of our pilgrimage was enjoyable and uneventful. Some time later I was talking to a priest friend who knew Assisi well. I told him of our experience at the bottom of the hill. He identified the exact spot and then proceeded to tell me that there had indeed been a wall there in the twelfth century. So, I thought to myself, Cecil wasn't hallucinating – just picking up a memory trace from the past.

I tell this story in some detail because it is very typical of psychic sensitivity. An apparently sensible, normal middle-aged woman sees something that no one else around her perceives. To an observant friend she seems to show signs of a mild trance-like state, even though she is still able to talk sense and to continue her journey. What is a little unusual about this story is that there was some objective confirmation of my friend's experience. What I believe happened was that Cecil somehow tuned into the twelfth century and picked up a strong memory trace of a wall. Something unpleasant may have happened there, and communicated itself to her as a warning that I was in some danger.

The experience that I have just described happened to a friend who I would call a 'sensitive', that is someone with a well-developed psychic sense. It is a natural gift, rather like that possessed by water diviners. Water diviners are able to perceive the presence of water deep under the earth. They can sometimes provide accurate information about its depth and quality. Those of us who do not possess this ability to dowse for water may feel somewhat mystified by their skills, but the evidence of their competence is so strong that we cannot deny it. An experienced practitioner, Tom Graves, has said that anyone can dowse:

> It's just a skill, which like any other can be learnt with practice, awareness and a working knowledge of its basic principles and mechanics.[2]

Both he and Lyall Watson, who has documented some of the fascinating evidence about dowsing and map dowsing (that is dowsing at a distance using a map), say that the ability to divine the presence of water is focused in a person's hands. It is not a task done by the twig, pendulum or other instrument. Rather it is the person's hands that transmit information to the brain. The mind analyses and decodes the message, and interprets its meaning.

If we can accept the hypothesis that the ability to pick up 'vibrations' from the past and the capacity to dowse for water are functions of the human body and mind we shall not be tempted to think of these skills as weird, magical or supernatural, any more than we now think of radio and television waves as mysterious. They are in the air all around us. We do not hear or see them until they are focused through a receiver, a radio or television set. So it is with human beings. All of us probably have the innate ability to pick up memory traces or find water under the ground, but some of us seem to have super-sensitive antennae, and can pick up information that is not available to other people

Using Psychic Gifts for Healing

Once you are able to accept the existence of these skills in regard to memory traces and water dowsing, it is easier to think about other skills which can be used by some people in the service of others. In the last chapter I spoke briefly about people who seem to be able to make diagnoses by putting their hands on a sick person. They are able to 'feel' where the sickness is, what it is and whether or not it is curable in the sense of a restoration to functional health. One could almost say they have the skill of dowsing for disease.[3] Now I need to say a bit about how such things actually feel because I think this whole area of healing needs demystifying.

Gifted Hands

Quite a large number of people have the innate capacity to 'feel' through their hands. You might be one of them, and if you are, you might be encouraged to know that such an ability is to be welcomed rather than feared.

If you read a lot of books about healing you will soon find out that many people who exercise a healing ministry have these gifts. Some of them become very well known indeed, but others, like myself, subsume their gifts in their professional role and are spared the dangers of publicity, at least during their working lives. Our accounts of what it feels like to diagnose through our hands are remarkably similar, yet the strange thing is that, until it happens to you, you don't quite believe it. Well, I certainly didn't.

I was very sceptical as a young doctor, full of the latest scientific knowledge and somewhat scornful of anyone who took the paranormal seriously. My medical diagnoses were strictly logical. Sometimes patients told me that I had 'comforting' or 'warm' hands when I touched them, and they didn't just mean that my hands were warm. But I had reached middle age before I knew I had this gift. Strangely, once I recognised its presence I realised I had always had it.

I haven't always used my hands consciously. There was virtually no need to do so when I was an active medical practitioner. Other gifts, such as knowledge, common sense and increasing experience, were all I needed on most occasions. But even then, sometimes (especially for those with whom I was closely linked in prayer) I did ask my hands to inform my mind, provided that the person who was seeking my help understood what I was doing and was willing for me to do this. Now that I am no longer a practising doctor I use my hands a lot, especially in connection with the Christian healing ministry.

Before I say what it feels like to use one's hands for diagnosis, I must make it clear that this gift cannot replace the proper skills of diagnostic medicine. It is a complementary gift, not a substitute. Moreover, the gift is not confined to Christians. It should not be confused with the gift of faith, nor with spiritual discernment, about which I shall be speaking in the next chapter. It is a natural ability, no more. No one taught it to me. I'm not sure it can be learnt, though I think an innate ability can be enhanced by training and experience.

Usually I begin by putting both hands lightly on the person's head. Then I relax and wait. I know that when I do this I go into a slightly 'far away' ruminative state of mind. I'm certainly not in a trance, nor am I drowsy. On the contrary, I'm very alert, but I'm attentive to an inner pool of stillness rather than to external noise or thoughts of any kind. Indeed, if thoughts come in at this stage I might as well stop, and often do. For I know that I am unlikely to reach the wordless place to which I need to go if this way of using my hands is going to work well. If, however, I do reach that state of quiet inner attentiveness and stay there for a few minutes, a prompting may come to my mind. Sometimes I feel a need to move my hands to another part of the body; sometimes I have a very strong, quietly insistent, single thought that comes to the surface. It might lead me to ask my client a question, or to enquire as to what is going on inside his or her mind and emotions.

Often there is no need for me to do anything. The client just tells me what is wrong. Suddenly, for instance, a man may know why his back is hurting; a woman may be given a tremendous insight into the reason why her marriage is going wrong. Something in the contact between us has released those individuals into a state where their own vision is clear. If something like this occurs, I will usually return to the stillness and wait again. As soon as I am sure that nothing more is going to enter the space I have left for it, I stop and return to our usual verbal relationship.

Personally, I always check the 'messages' I get in this way against information from other sources. I realise that I may be wrong. I may have got my wires crossed and be on the wrong tack altogether. I may be moving in the right direction, but stop too soon to hear the truth God wants me to hear. I'm also well aware that in my slight state of disassociation I may pick up facts that are not strictly relevant to the person who has entrusted themselves to me, and I'll explain what I mean by that later on in this chapter.

When using my hands in this way I do not suspend my scientific or medical judgement at all. Instead I use my 'hunch' to help me explore possible diagnoses I had not previously thought very much about. Quite often the combination of 'hunch', knowledge, reason and experience leads to the correct diagnosis of the problem.

This way of using my hands has been most helpful in a variety of situations, and there has been little difference between physical, emotional and spiritual problems. What does seem to make a difference is whether or not the client has sufficient trust in me to allow themselves to be open (in other words, willing for me to enter their psychic space). I do not for a moment blame them if they can't allow me to do so. It can be quite alarming to find yourself unexpectedly exposing your secret thoughts and pains to another person.

If, then, you have gifted hands, remember it *is* a gift, a present to you from nature; one that can be used for the benefit of other people, but one that carries with it certain responsibilities and some dangers too. I shall discuss those shortly, but for now I want to turn to another gift, the gift of knowledge.

The Gift of Knowledge

My friend Cecil, with whom I went to Assisi, had the gift of knowledge about the past. She saw a wall and knew there was danger associated with it. Many other people have had similar experiences. Some see ghosts. Some just know that something terrible happened in a particular place. Some can discern exactly what did happen; others can't. They just feel terribly cold and afraid in certain places. This kind of gift works in the opposite direction too. Many people are able to find special places where there are 'good vibes', as they say, a feeling of peace, harmony and warmth.

I have known many places like this. When I was six years old I found a quiet field in Sussex, close to a clifftop overlooking the English Channel. It was a place of happiness and safety, a kind of secret haven. I returned to it again and again as I grew into adulthood. I last went there just after my husband died and it still gave me that kind of feeling.

If you know a peaceful and healing place yourself, treasure it. If you want to look for such places, you'll often find them in the crypts of very old churches and cathedrals. I suspect that 'upstairs' in the main body of the church there is too much traffic, too many people on their way through, for a place to acquire this kind of numinous peace, but 'downstairs', where the dead sometimes lie close at hand, you will often find a healing sense of stillness and strength.

People do not necessarily interfere with the numinous. Famous shrines, like Lourdes, Fatima, Walsingham and Glastonbury, attract thousands of pilgrims who find the healing they need. Places like Little Gidding near Huntingdon, where 'prayer has been valid',[4] and many monasteries and convents, are also places where you are likely to find these 'good vibes'. If you know where to go, you can always find strength, peace and joy, even when you are all upside down emotionally.

These good places are marvellous to discover, but there are also places which are troubled by bad memory traces, places where things like murder or rape happened, places that were inhabited by evil men and women. People with the gift of knowledge can be troubled by such memory traces and can sometimes become quite unwell. They are often afraid and are more likely to be helped by attending to their fear, rather than by becoming preoccupied with its exact cause. Having said that, it is also true that the ministry of deliverance has its place in the treatment of places and people who are haunted by the past. Such matters are beyond the scope of this book, but anyone who seriously feels oppressed by a sense of evil which is coming from the past needs to get help from a reputable minister of religion and a good doctor.

So much for the past. But what about knowledge of the present and the future? What about clairvoyance and clairaudience? These gifts of knowledge are outside the range of the so-called normal; that is to say relatively few people in any community possess this gift. It is often thought that clairvoyance and clairaudience have to do with the future, but that is not necessarily so. Clairvoyance literally means 'clear seeing' and may be used to describe abnormally clear insight or perception. Clairaudient people seem to have the same gift but they hear things outside the normal range. Such 'sensitive' people literally know or hear one's thoughts and often see one's life laid out before them. These gifts do not necessarily depend on physical contact.

Some people can discern a person's present life in some detail, and even foretell the future. I suspect that some fortune-tellers have this gift, especially if they have Romany blood, or if the gift is in their family's genes, so to speak. It is a very uncomfortable gift, because the fact that you can 'see' a person's life does not necessarily mean that you have the right or duty to reveal what you 'see'.

I know this from personal experience, for both my mother and an aunt on my mother's side had the gift and I have it too. I very seldom reveal what I know or use the knowledge I have acquired. Nor do I 'look', except in exceptional circumstances and with someone's permission. I will normally want to have their complete trust before consciously using this gift, and I also need to be able to trust myself with the knowledge I may acquire. Quite a lot of doctors and priests seem to have this gift and maybe it has something to do with their professional needs. I don't know. What I do know is that it is a dangerous gift because it can be so easily misused.

Sometimes I see what I don't want to see, but sometimes I see what I need to see. It is what I do with the information that matters. I have spoken about the dangers of having gifted hands and to this I must now add a word of caution about the gift of knowledge. Indeed, there are many dangers in having this particular gift.

Some Hazards of Psychic Sensitivity

Psychic gifts can and often do give one power over other people, particularly if the gift is strong. One's hands or clear-sightedness can be used to discern and tell other people things it would be wiser not to tell. Alternatively, because one already knows the answers, one might conduct an interview in such a way as to force someone to a distressing and premature real-isation of the insolubility of his or her problem. If I were a patient I would be very cautious indeed about consulting a clairvoyant or clairaudient, especially if I were inclined to be a bit psychic myself. Such people are easier to 'read', and more open to exploitation and abuse for that reason. To begin with, this is a field where charlatans abound. Secondly, one may not be sufficiently aware of one's own vulnerability: the knowledge that the clairvoyant is imparting may be too much to bear. I have, for instance, known people pushed to the point of suicide by the indiscreet use of clairvoyant knowledge.

No one has a right to walk into anyone's innermost thoughts and space. If you find people doing this without your request or consent, you would be wise to avoid close contact with them. This may seem a strong warning, but it is based on experience.

Psychic sensitivity is a gift that enables its owners to speak with authority, and authority confers power. Power itself is morally neutral, but some people who have it unfortunately lay claim to it themselves rather than rendering it to God from whom all authority and power derive. If healers are prone to this error their clients are even more likely to fall into it. I have found that men and women alike can easily become dependent on people who have what appears to be an unusual gift. Healers who need to be needed are sometimes trapped by their own desire to help everyone at all times and in all places. They can sometimes respond to a client's distress by appearing to have 'knowledge' when in fact none has been given to them on that particular occasion. These healers are not dishonest. They have just been seduced by their need to be needed.

Another rather terrible consequence of having this gift is that it is all too easy to manipulate people emotionally by a fine display of one's abilities. Healers who do a lot of their work at public services know this danger very well, and most of them try to avoid it, but there is something about a crowd of people together that makes them behave very differently from when they are acting as individuals. In their heightened susceptibility to emotion they become very vulnerable to mass hysteria. I have undoubedly seen this at some healing services I have attended. Although great good can be done by such services, notwithstanding their highly charged emotional temperature, I have also seen harm done to people who were carried away at the time and thought they were cured when they were not.

I can, for instance, recall an epileptic patient who went to such a service. The clairvoyant healer told him sufficient detail about his family and life history to seduce him into complete trust. On being declared cured of his affliction, he threw away all his anti-convulsant drugs. The next time I saw him, he had had a severe epileptic fit. He had fallen into an open fire and had been badly burnt. These kinds of ill effects can largely be avoided by the provision of careful counselling at healing services and good pastoral care afterwards. If there had been someone qualified to take a detailed history from this epileptic patient, and someone to do follow-up visits, he might have been spared much pain and the healers might have learnt some wisdom. I have been to healing services where these provisions are made, so it is possible to find such care.

In saying this, I do not discount the beneficial effects of catharsis, of releasing powerful emotions in a concentrated period of time. I have seen African witch doctors working themselves and a large group of people into ecstasy over a period of hours. When all were exhausted they collapsed in a heap on the ground. When they recovered it was as if they had been cleansed and purified by their experiences to such an extent that they felt calm and well, full of energy and beneficence towards their neighbours, at any rate for a time. Although I have not been present at Muslim services where dervishes achieve collective ecstasy through whirling dances and ritual chanting I believe this too is cathartic. Similarly, it seems likely that the sects which use venomous snakes in their ecstatic dances work in the same way.

Rituals of any kind, especially religious ones, can be very beneficial. The symbolic actions of the ritual have a deep psychological effect upon the participants, as those of us who love highly ritualised church services know. Well thought out healing services which make use of this kind of symbolic action are very effective.

I shall say more about charismatic healing in the next chapter because it claims to be direct healing by the Holy Spirit. Charismatic healing services should be and usually are Spirit-filled, but they are also attended by the dangers of extreme emotionalism. It is possible for Christian healers and congregations alike to be misled into dependence on catharsis rather than on the Holy Spirit. I am not against these services, but I think their dangers need to be noted. I also have to say that all the Christian healers I know take great trouble to avoid these dangers and to point people to God as the source of all healing rather than to themselves.

Apart from power, there are other dangers too, mainly those

associated with error. It is very easy to make mistakes in this field of work. This is partly because of the close relationship between 'knowledge' and telepathy. Telepathy is another natural gift. It is the transference of one person's thoughts to another. Despite thousands of scientific experiments the existence of telepathy has not been proven, but many people, including myself, are convinced that it does happen.[5]

Telepathy can undoubtedly get in the way of true knowledge. I remember, for instance, once working closely with a priest. I was a very young doctor at the time. He was a very experienced priest. We were both people of some integrity in our own fields. The priest knew a great deal about black magic. I knew nothing about it at all. I am quite certain that I had never read anything about satanism at the time. Suddenly in the course of our work together I found myself describing an unpleasant ritual. The detail was accurate. The priest assumed that I must have had personal experience of the ritual. He was wrong. I did not. I had probably picked up his thoughts by telepathy and simply relayed them back to him. That kind of experience can be unpleasant and counter-productive. I would certainly never make any assumptions about anyone on the basis of such slender evidence. Telepathy has no therapeutic benefit – I only mention it because it is sometimes confused with the gift of knowledge and observation.

Many people can appear to read thoughts, especially when they are physically close to one another. This is not telepathy. It is the gift of observation, which is almost subconscious. Most of us do it by close observation of the little unconscious signals that people invariably give out. Rightly used, it can be a source of great comfort and healing to someone that you instinctively know what they are feeling. Such empathy is valuable and should never be despised. As with all the gifts I have been describing, it is the integrity of the healer or friend that matters.

The Reverend Dr Martin Israel, who is an Anglican priest and doctor of medicine, has written extensively about psychic gifts and about healing and healers. In one of his most important books, *The Quest for Wholeness*, he points out that the character of the person who has psychic gifts is of the utmost importance if he or she is engaged in any healing ministry. He says:

> In no field is the wariness of the serpent and the innocence of the dove (to quote Matthew 10:16) as necessary as in healing work, because irrespective of the minister's spiritual allegiance, there is a strong involvement of psychic forces in the operations. It seems that the Holy Spirit works through the vast angelic hosts as well as the Communion of Saints; according to the person's character, he is likely to draw to himself the corresponding intermediary agents: a selfish disposition brings him close to the forces of evil, whereas a selfless one will draw him to the powers of light that illuminate his path and direct him in the way of resurrection. We do not need to command the forces in the intermediate psychic zone; all that is required of us is a purity of intent that allows the forces of light to enter and transfigure us as a preliminary to our healing work with others on the way.[6]

So far I have been talking about psychic gifts: gifts that seem to me to belong to the natural order of creation, gifts that are widespread and often well developed among those engaged in healing work on behalf of others. Although there are some dangers in having them, these gifts, as I have tried to show, are God-given and good. They are not restricted to men and women of faith, nor are they only to be found among Christians. Nevertheless, all through this chapter I have been conscious that psychic gifts carry with them a slight sense of the extraordinary. They can sometimes display themselves in a quite dramatic way. Although I have tried to show how quietly and sensibly such gifts can be used in ordinary life I am also aware that my focus on 'sensitivity' may seem to detract from the role of faith in healing. So, let me say at once that I believe all the psychic gifts in the world count for nothing compared with the gift of faith. It is to the role of faith in healing that I now turn.

CHAPTER FIVE

Touching the Spiritual

Look well, O soul, upon yourself
lest spiritual ambition
should mislead and blind you
to your essential task –
to wait in quietness:
to knock and persevere in humble faith.

Gilbert Shaw (1886–1967)[1]

When I was working as a general medical practitioner I met a remarkable woman who had many psychic gifts. She was also a devout spiritualist who attended her local church every Sunday. She was a medium; that is she acted as a kind of go-between for people who wanted to be in touch with their dead relatives.

Alice, as I will call her here, had a number of spirit guides who talked through her. I suppose that in her own spiritualist church Alice would do most of her work in a light trance state, but I never saw any sign of altered consciousness in her at any time during the ten years that we knew each other.

Going to visit Alice on account of some minor but incapacitating illness was a fascinating adventure. I would arrive and sit down and carry on a very ordinary conversation with her about her health. Sometimes, but not always, our talk would be abruptly interrupted by the arrival of one of Alice's numerous friends from 'the other side'. Alice would greet them warmly and proceed to carry on an animated conversation in my presence.

'Sorry, dear,' she'd say to me. 'They're so eager to give me their messages; they can't wait for the proper time.'

'I wonder why they come when I come?' I said one day, when there seemed to be more talk with them than with me!

'Oh, they like you,' Alice replied. 'You're in the same line of business, aren't you?'

At the time I thought Alice was talking about the fact that I was a doctor, but she wasn't. I asked her what she meant and was startled by her reply.

'You're a Christian, aren't you?' she said. 'You believe in the resurrection of the dead, don't you? And in the Communion of Saints?'

'Yes.'

'You pray to Jesus?'

'Yes.'

'And to the saints?'

'Yes.'

'Well then, you speak to them in the depths of your heart. I do too. Don't tell me you don't expect answers, because I know you do sometimes get them.'

'Well, yes,' I said, 'but not like that, not with dead souls who come to you when you're in a trance and speak through you to people. Jesus and the saints don't give me messages in seances.'

Alice gave one of her enigmatic smiles. 'You're in the same line of business,' she said. 'You have the healing gift, only you don't want to know that, or to say so.'

She was more then half right. In her kindly way Alice had challenged my faith. She had also suggested that I wasn't using my God-given gifts as I should

I respected Alice; she had reciprocated by sending her organically ill clients to one or other of the doctors in our practice. Her spiritual authority was impressive. I could not say the same of all spiritualists, nor of all Christians. There are charlatans in every religious sect, and misguided do-gooders who think they know everything when they know nothing. There are people who make a good living out of our gullibility. Of course there are. That does not mean to say we should condemn all doctors and healers and others who are different in some way from us.

It so happened that my conversation with Alice took place

75

during my period of disillusionment with healing, after that disastrous encounter with a healer at the bedside of a dying child. It was before I had seen the best side of the Christian healing ministry, so I had a lot of work to do.

The first thing I did was to try to get rid of some of my prejudices about certain spiritualists and Christians, mostly those more outgoing and ebullient healers who seem so prominent in the charismatic and evangelical branches of the Church. As I gradually acquired a little tolerance and humility, and weeded out some of my preconceptions about faith healing, especially the Christian kind, I found a lot of my own reservations disappearing. But I still just wanted to remain a sensible, moderately good, ordinary, traditional Christian general medical practitioner.

It was while I was ruminating about these matters that I got two other jolts, or as I prefer to think of them, messages from God. The first arrived in the shape of a woman patient whom I'll call Sarah. I had been looking after her for a long time. She had a chronic backache which I thought was related to some stress at home. I had more or less given up hope of it getting better. Sarah used to come and see me once a month for a few pain-killers and the medical certificate that enabled her to stay off work. That morning she came in as usual. I looked up, greeted her and pulled the pad of medical certificates towards me.

'I don't need one, thank you, Doctor. I can go back to work.'

'How come?' I said.

'I went to see the faith healer,' she said, in a tone that left no room for further enquiry.

'Well, if you're sure?' I said. I was too dumbfounded to say anything else. Besides, I was offended. There was I, a good practising Christian. Why did Sarah have to take herself off to a faith healer down the road? It was too much for me to take lying down, but I said nothing.

'Yes. Yes, thank you. I'm fine now. I'm sorry you couldn't help me,' she added. She must have sensed my chagrin, poor soul.

Sarah departed happily. I saw her a few months later on another matter and she was still well and happy.

The second jolt came from a dying patient, whom I'll call John, who came to tell me that he was going to Lourdes on pilgrimage.

'I know I'll be healed,' he said.

I glanced at him. He looked terribly ill. He was in a lot of pain and we hadn't been able to control it very well. I looked across at his wife. She and I both knew he had only a few weeks left to live.

'He wants to go so much,' she said. 'The people who run the Jumbulance[2] say it'll be all right. We'll only be away for a few days.'

'Why not?' I said. 'I hope you'll feel better.' It was an inane remark to make. I hadn't yet learned the wisdom of holding my tongue.

After their return from Lourdes, I was called to their home. John still looked terribly ill but the pain had gone out of his face. He looked serene. Jane, his wife, was glowing.

'It's wonderful,' she said. 'I've never seen him like this, not since the beginning of the illness. We've talked about his dying. We've laughed together. We've been happy – really happy.'

John died peacefully a few weeks later. He never again had the kind of agonising pain he had previously suffered. All the mental anguish had disappeared. Lourdes had worked its miracle.

Both Sarah's story and John's are true. I have altered the details a little. That is all. What both episodes did for me was to help me appreciate the importance of faith in their lives. As a result I looked again at my own beliefs, especially in regard to the role of faith in healing.

I started by going back to the Bible, where I rediscovered Jesus the healer.[3] I began to take the Christian healing ministry seriously. And then, as I have already said, I met Harry Potts. I soon found that I could no longer stay outside the Church's ministry and I began to pray the prayer of faith.

All that happened many years ago. What I say now springs directly from my Christian experience, so if the language seems a little foreign, I hope you will re-interpret it in the light of your own faith and experience. Or use it as a stepping stone to a deeper understanding of your own beliefs and attitudes towards healing.

Christians go to see their doctors. They trust surgeons with their lives. They visit psychiatrists, herbalists, acupuncturists. In short they behave like everyone else. But they also rely on the prayer of faith, on each other's healing ministries, on the sacraments and on the ministries of deliverance from evil. I propose to look at each of these in turn.

The Prayer of Faith

> You need not cry very loud. He is nearer to us than we are aware of.
>
> Brother Lawrence (1605–1691)[4]

I am a woman of faith. My creed is very simple. I believe in God who is Love. I live in that Love and shall die into that Love, and nothing, but nothing, can separate me from that Love. Even terrible disasters and personal suffering haven't been able to get in the way of that belief.

I also believe in Jesus Christ, God's son, who rescues me from the consequences of my sins and who shows me the way to live my life as his disciple. I follow him as closely as I can by trying to live my life according to his example and teachings.

I do this with the help of the Holy Spirit who is invisibly present in God's world and who 'is nearer to me than I am aware of'. The Holy Spirit guides me into truth and gives me help through the Church – the whole Company of the Saints living and dead – to remain faithful to my calling as a Christian disciple.

Essentially that is my faith. I have also learnt about the doctrines and traditions of my own particular part of the Christian Church, but they are not as important to me as my passionate belief in God who is Love, who teaches me how to love and who gives me the strength I need to follow in the way of love.

Love, that is to say God, keeps our love for each other alive through prayer which the Holy Spirit initiates from the depths of our being. My own prayer, like my faith, is very simple. It just consists in waiting 'in quietness', as Father Gilbert Shaw puts it in the prayer at the beginning of this chapter; 'in knocking and in persevering in humble faith'. That is to say it isn't just waiting. It's a way of waiting – in quietness of soul – in complete confidence that God hears my prayer for myself and for others. I trust that the prayer will be answered even if I can't always understand or welcome the answer.

Moreover, the prayer of faith is not just a passive acquiescence in a pre-determined fate over which I have no control. It is true that I want God to be in control, not I. I also know that my part is to knock on God's door and to persevere in that knocking. Father Shaw's prayer is about seeking wholeness. It goes on:

> Knock; knock in love,
> nor fail to keep your place before the door
> that when Christ wills – and not before –
> he may open unto you the treasures of his love.[5]

So I try to keep my place 'before the door' and wait in hope for 'the treasures of his love'.

There are a thousand different ways of praying. What matters is that each person finds a way that is comfortable for him or her. There is no right way. There is only God's way for you. It sometimes helps to know what other people do and there are a host of books about praying for healing which might help at some stage in your own journey of faith. But for now, let me tell you just a few of the ways I pray this simple prayer of faith, in relation to God's healing work.

Praying Alone

> Whenever you pray, go into your room and shut the door and pray to your Father who is in secret; and your Father who sees in secret will reward you.[6]

79

Jesus often went off by himself to pray. He told his disciples to do the same. I suspect that when we begin to pray 'in secret' a lot of our prayer is a mixture of 'thank you' and 'please'. After all most of us have been brought up to be polite to our 'elders and betters', so it seems appropriate to treat God as if he were a rather rich but slightly unpredictable grandfather. 'Thank you' comes before and after 'please', as all small children know. But it tends to be the 'please' that's uppermost in our minds when we pray the prayer of petition. When we intercede we ask God for what we need and want, both for ourselves and for others. It is quite all right to do that. God understands and loves us for it, and really doesn't mind us thinking that being rewarded means getting what we ask for. Sometimes we do indeed get that kind of reward but only, I'm sure, when it was in God's mind anyway. In my experience, it usually ends up in two quite challenging ways.

The first is that I begin to see God's point of view and that can sometimes be very different from my original thoughts on the matter. I, of course, always want everyone I pray for to be cured of whatever it is that ails them. I want their suffering to end as quickly as possible. God, on the other hand, seems to be able to use suffering as a means of someone's healing; not always, but sometimes. God sometimes doesn't seem too concerned about curing people, but always draws them towards wholeness.

This tension between my desire and God's loving purposes works away in me until I change. For instance, if I have a friend with cancer I might very well start off by praying for a complete cure. And that might happen. However, if it doesn't, then I might gradually come to ask that he or she be spared undue suffering, and be able to grow through it into final fulfilment of themselves in resurrection life. Eventually I might ask God to end that suffering with a merciful and swift death.

Of course, I know very well that it might not happen that way at all. I have had to watch many clients and friends go through humiliating experiences and terrible suffering on their way towards the end of their lives. Then I cry out to God in misery and rage; and God and I both understand my anger and accept it as a token of my love for my friends and patients.

Seeing God's point of view is not at all easy when what is happening to us, or to our relatives and friends, seems so cruel and unjust. Then it is very hard to see that any good can come out of suffering. It is at such times that I have nearly always been led by God to meet or to read about someone who has come through suffering and found healing in and through their prayer of faith. One such person who has helped me greatly is Joni Eareckson, a young American woman, who was paralysed when her neck was broken. She has written her autobiography, *Joni*, and many other books about her struggle to resist becoming warped by her suffering. She tells of how she eventually found that being paralysed was not the end of any worthwhile existence for her, but the beginning of a new life in Christ.[7]

Jennifer Rees Larcombe is another person who has taught me that suffering can be a transforming experience. Her book, *Beyond Healing*, is a moving account of her struggle with a rare viral disease which damages brain cells and nerve endings. Her illness put her into a wheelchair. It made it impossible for her to care adequately for her home or her six children. It made her irritable and at times of relapse she became very depressed. In her book, written when she was adjusting to the idea that she would never be cured of her illness, Jennifer gives a moving account of how her struggles against depression during a period of physical relapse changed her prayer:

> I can actually see the entries of my prayer diary changing in nature. At first they were screams for help and deliverance, then endless little personal requests like, 'Lord show me what to wear today,' and 'What shall I cook for tea?' People in depression are totally turned in on themselves. They cannot help it; it is a symptom of the illness, like spots with measles, but after a while I found myself praying for Tony and the children. Then as I forced myself to make contact again with other people, I began

to be concerned for their needs and prayed about their problems, a sure sign I was on the mend. Finally one morning I wrote, 'Lord I *seem* to come to You each morning with a list of things *I want you to do for me or others.* Please help me to ask you first what You want *me* to do for *You.*'[8]

Jennifer is describing her gradual recovery from the profoundly debilitating condition of depression. I think she is also recording something that happens whenever we pray with integrity. As we listen to God we find ourselves being drawn more deeply into God's way of working in our lives. So we begin to change. What happened to Jennifer was that she started to look outwards. What has often happened to me is that I begin to feel some real responsibility towards the person I am praying for. This is the second creative thing that comes out of the prayer of faith when one really tries to listen to God.

Time and again I find that the Holy Spirit asks me what I'm going to do to help with the healing. Then I find myself encouraged to take specific action. One particular example of how the Holy Spirit works stands out in my mind.

One of my closest friends, Kath, was dying of cancer. In all the time I had known her as a well woman Kath's faith had been wonderfully strong. Now, under the impact of brain secondaries, she had apparently lost that precious gift. Some mutual friends had been to see her. They had come back terribly distressed by their encounter with a bitter Kath who was rejecting all Christian ministry. They asked me to go and see what I could do.

I found myself making excuses. There were some genuine reasons for my procrastination, but the truth was that I was afraid of how I would react to my friend's terrible spiritual desolation. Only I didn't know that at the time.

That night I settled down to pray for Kath's healing. As I tried to listen to God, the Holy Spirit began to whisper in the ear of my soul. By the end of my prayer time I knew very well that God was not content with my 'prayer-at-a-distance' as far as Kath was concerned. The next morning I rearranged my day off and used it to go and visit her.

It was the beginning of an extraordinary phase in our relationship which lasted until her death some weeks later. Kath continued to refuse all outward Christian ministry. She had been a devout Roman Catholic so this was quite upsetting to her Catholic friends. I was not a Roman Catholic, and that may have been why she made fewer efforts to drive me away. At any rate, she welcomed my visits. I would sit and hold her hand. No words passed between us, at least none that I wanted to speak and none that she might have wanted to hear before the cancer attacked her brain. It was as if the Holy Spirit was closing my lips: and yet I'm convinced that something very healing was happening for both of us during my visits.

When Kath died I was profoundly grateful to God for the way in which God had worked in my soul during those weeks. In and through her very woundedness she had brought me one step closer to wholeness. I was, and am, thankful for that encounter with the Holy Spirit during my prayer of intercession.

I don't think it matters how you pray alone, as long as you do. Personally, I don't use lists of people to pray for. I simply rely on the Holy Spirit to put them into my mind. I don't know what happens when I pray, nor how God uses the energy of my love for the person I am praying for or with. I just believe God wants me to care enough to go on praying and listening and getting involved in the Holy Spirit's plans. Again, Jennifer Rees Larcombe's story strengthens my personal convictions about this. She prayed alone, but she also prayed in company.

Praying in Company

> Where two or three are gathered in my name, I am there among them.[9]

In June 1990 a young, recently converted Christian woman found herself at a healing prayer meeting in Guildford at which Jennifer Rees Larcombe was the main speaker. The young woman sat in the front row. At the end of Jennifer's talk and just before the lunch break, this young woman found herself standing up. She told Jennifer that, 'God is saying He wants to heal you.'

Now Jennifer had prayed for healing for many years and her desire for a cure had never been granted. Many experienced Christian elders and ministers had laid hands on her, and thousands of Christians had prayed for her. Jennifer had gone a long way towards being healed, but she had more or less given up expecting to be cured, although, as she says in her own account, since March 1990 God had been telling her she would be cured by an unexpected source. As she saw her stand up, Jennifer 'knew' that she would be cured through this young, inexperienced woman's ministry.

After some initial reluctance the young woman was persuaded to pray for Jennifer. She did so in a very simple way. Jennifer says:

> She did not do any of the things the books on healing say you ought to do, and neither did I! She simply asked Jesus to heal me and he did! I was not slain in the Spirit. I felt no warmth or excitement. I simply knew I was completely well.[10]

Jennifer got out of her wheelchair immediately. She was well. Her sudden cure has not been without its problems, but it has held. It has brought her new responsibilities: those attached to being a well woman who no longer needs help, who no longer needs a disability pension, who no longer commands sympathy. She no longer enjoys an instant rapport with former fellow-sufferers. She is separated from them by the fact that she has been cured, whereas they have not been restored to functional health.[11] Yes, there are problems about being well and I shall speak of them again in the last chapter of this book, but meanwhile I want to look at some more of the many ways of praying in company.

Many Christians never pray for healing in company. There are all sorts of reasons for this. Sometimes it's embarrassment;

sometimes a reticence about bothering God with one's own small troubles; sometimes apathy; sometimes, I think, a deep-seated suspicion that prayer doesn't accomplish anything. Even if we do pray with conviction, we often say to ourselves: 'After all if God really is "in charge", is there much point in trying to change God's mind?' Lastly it seems to me that sometimes we don't go to pray with others because we are so terribly aware of our own feebleness and we think everyone else's prayers are much more effective than our own! We know that may be nonsense, but that's how we feel. These kinds of internal conversations go on in most of us, including myself, but in answer to all of them I would say, 'Try it and see.'

There are Christian healing groups all over the world and all of them are based on Jesus' promise to be present 'where two or three are gathered'. The fellowship of Jesus 'in the midst' has to be experienced to be believed. You can find that sense of the living presence of Jesus in a Christian home, in a parish room attached to a church, inside the church itself, in a pilgrimage to Lourdes or Walsingham or simply in some place that is made holy by its closeness to God. You will even find it in the group you have joined.

One of the most encouraging true stories I have come across shows just how important it is to be able to turn to a local prayer group in time of need. In 1989 Christine Pincott had a Caesarean section after a difficult pregnancy and complicated early labour. Her husband, David, was with her and saw their daughter, Kate, born. After her birth David was unexpectedly asked to leave. He sensed there was something wrong, and his fears were confirmed when the consultant obstetrician told him that Christine had a large secondary cancer in her liver. The primary focus was a tiny, hitherto undetected, cancer in one breast.

Christine knew nothing of this at the time. She made an initial recovery but then went into kidney failure. David had called his local pastor as soon as he had been told the bad news. They had prayed together and a minister from their fellowship had anointed Christine with oil. All the members of their local church, together with a much wider network of Christians from other churches, began to pray fervently for Christine. The following day her kidneys began to work again. She was given chemotherapy and made a good recovery. However, a year later she fell ill with abdominal pains. It was feared that she might have a recurrence of the liver cancer, but an exploratory operation showed that the problem was caused by scar tissue on her bowel. Her liver looked normal. Subsequent scans were also clear and although she still goes to the hospital for three-monthly checks, and knows the cancer might yet return, she also feels that 'the Lord's healing of me was something of a miracle'. She says:

> The amazing thing was that I had no surgery . . . all that was left in my breast was a little deposit of calcium . . . I think these things happen in life [qv Chapter 3], but the Lord used my experience to bring me closer to him and he has brought tremendous good out of the whole episode . . . It has made me realise that God is deeper than the deepest pit. I know it because I've been there . . . I think however that I would have died without the prayer support. It was people's prayers that saved me . . .[12]

Christine and David are still prayed for regularly. They now belong to South West London Vineyard Church, which is connected with John Wimber in the USA. If Christine's cancer does return, will they feel 'let down' by their Lord or by their church? I doubt it. John Wimber was the pastor and evangelist who ministered to a well-known evangelical Christian, David Watson, who died from his cancer despite intensive prayer. He had shown an excellent initial response, and his relapse was a tremendous disappointment to many people who had been praying for him. But not to him. Nineteen days before he died David Watson said, 'I am completely at peace – there is nothing that I want more than to go to heaven. I know how good it is.'[13] He died on 18 February 1984 and his work lives on. So too does the faith – in the Vineyard Church and among Christians everywhere. So it would be, one instinctively feels, with Christine and David Pincott and their family and friends.

One of the best things about healing prayer groups for me has been the strength of fellowship; a strength that isn't dependent on any of us as individuals but on God who is there in and beyond us all. I know that if I'm burdened by a heaviness of heart in relation to someone I'm praying for, I will be able to share that burden without breaking any confidences. I also know that if I need healing myself I can trust a group of friends I have come to know well through praying with them on a regular basis.

Healing prayer groups vary in size from 'prayer couples' or 'triplets' to groups of eight to twelve. They can be attached to a particular church or be inter-denominational. I don't know of any inter-faith groups, but that's not to say they don't exist. It's a question of looking around locally for what you need and if you can't find it looking further afield.

Some people don't find it easy to pray in small groups. They prefer to go to a more anonymous healing service. Many churches now hold these healing services, usually once a month, or once a quarter. At these services there is praise, singing, listening to the word of God, intercession and then often the laying on of hands for healing. Ministers of religion and trained lay people usually officiate. Members of the congregation may receive the healing ministry for themselves or for those for whom they are praying. To receive the laying on of hands for another person is quite usual. It is called absent healing and it is based upon the belief that God can heal at a distance, as Jesus did when he healed the centurion's servant.[14]

Such healing services may or may not be helpful to you personally. Again it's a matter of trying it out for a reasonable length of time so that you can make an informed judgement. It is better not to rely entirely on first impressions, even if you have one or two initial experiences which are not immediately helpful. No one who goes to such a service is ever forced to ask for the laying on of hands if they don't feel that it is the right time for them to have this particular ministry.

At some healing services, anointing with oil is also offered. Anointing with oil is a very ancient Christian practice which is especially commended where one is conscious of disease, discomfort or unhappiness due to sin (one's own or other people's). It is a very simple rite. After the laying on of hands, another minister comes to each person with specially blessed oil and traces the sign of the cross on their foreheads and on the outstretched palms of their hands. As we have physical bodies, God honours us by using material gifts from creation to be the vehicles of our healing. Most of the healing services I have ever been to have been very peaceful and joyful; and sometimes they have been quite exuberant.

Many people are interested to know what the difference is between an ordinary healing service and a charismatic one. In one sense, I believe there is no difference, for the Holy Spirit brings strengthening help and healing to people at every kind of healing service. At ordinary services those gifts come quietly. At most charismatic services – especially when God's outpouring is expected, as it is by those who attend such services – the Holy Spirit's presence is marked by excitement, emotional release and ecstasy. People sing, dance, clap, and raise their hands in honour of God. The gifts seem to descend in profusion and to be experienced by a number of people at the same time. There are a variety of gifts: words of wisdom and knowledge; faith; healings; miracles; prophecies; discernment of spirits; various kinds of 'tongues' (a kind of babbling, often in a meaningless or strange language); and interpretation of tongues.[15] The laying on of hands may be accompanied by emotion and sometimes quite noisy rejoicing.

If you haven't been to such a service before, you may well find it difficult to cope with. Your feelings should be respected, but it is also worth remembering that to receive the Holy Spirit's outpouring of love *is* an overwhelming experience. Indeed, some people are 'slain in the Spirit'; that is they feel so heavy that they cannot stand upright. They sink to the floor, or even fall to the ground, in what appears to be a faint. There is nothing very terrible about it. Those who attend charismatic

Water is the outward sign of Baptism; the consecrated bread and wine are the outward signs of the Eucharistic feast which takes place in the depths of our being. By Baptism we are healed from our sin; by Holy Communion we are made whole by our incorporation into God as we are nourished by bread and wine. Indeed, many Christians feel so healed by the sacrament of the Eucharist that they feel there is no need for anything else. They regard the laying on of hands or anointing with oil as superfluous additions. On the other hand there are those who feel that when Christ comes into our bodies in the sacrament he frees us to be more open to receive God's healing, so they are happy to receive this ministry during a service of Holy Communion.

Baptism and the Eucharist are the two great sacraments of healing. Two others have importance in many people's lives – the sacraments of Reconciliation and Holy Unction – though some Christians do not recognise these as sacraments since they were not instituted by Christ during his lifetime.

The sacrament of Reconciliation involves open confession of sin to God in the presence of another person. In the Roman Catholic, Orthodox and Anglican churches this person has to be an ordained priest or bishop. In other churches any discreet and wise person may exercise this ministry. The rite of confession, which gives assurance of forgiveness for past sin, provides a symbolic means of restitution. Some people are greatly helped by confession: others, not at all. You need to decide what is right for you.

Holy Unction is used in connection with healing, often but not necessarily after confession. The rite is a little more elaborate than simple anointing at a healing service. The outward sign of anointing with oil is an expression of our confidence that we are inwardly healed by God.

People vary in temperament and disposition and if sacramental healing does not speak to your condition then it is best to stay away from it altogether.

Deliverance Healing

Deliver us from evil.[17]

Deliverance ministries hit the headlines from time to time, mostly when they go wrong! It is unfortunate when someone who is psychiatrically ill is wrongly considered to be possessed by demons. It is terrible when exorcisms go wrong. It is tragic when people commit suicide because they mistakenly believe that they are beyond redemption. These things do happen and when they do the newspapers have a field day.

When we read about such things we may find ourselves feeling quite critical of the unfortunate exorcists for their inept handling of the situation. It is all too easy to condemn other people, especially when they make an obvious mistake. It is also easy to dismiss the devil as a figment of some people's imaginations. Many people do just that. They may be right to be cautious about assigning personhood to the devil, for most of what we like to ascribe to the devil is more properly due to our own wickedness; but to refuse to acknowledge evil as a potential cause of illness is to fly in the face of the evidence.

I have deliberately refrained from discussing deliverance ministries in detail. I think far too much attention is paid to the devil. If you think the devil is 'prowling around' you,[18] the best thing to do is to make the sign of the cross and say the Lord's own prayer, 'Our Father', slowly and steadily. It is the best prayer to make for deliverance, and anyone can use it.

Evil cannot stand against God. Evil cannot gain entrance to our lives unless we allow it to. Those are the two important things to keep in mind when we are praying for deliverance from evil. If we command evil to depart in the name of Jesus Christ the evil *will* depart – providing that we aren't being half-hearted about it and at the same time toying with the thought of allowing him reign in our lives. If we tell a demon to go to the place which God has prepared for it that demon will obey. If it doesn't and we, or the people we are helping, go on being tempted to sin then we or they may need help from an experienced minister or priest. This should be someone who is

91

used to the ways of evil, but who can also build up our strength so that we can resist all the temptations that evil may put in our paths. Such experienced people can usually be found through one's local parish priest or minister of religion. Each denomination has a network of people who are trained and authorised to do this work.

When I ask myself why the Christian healing ministries are so important to me I come up with a rather surprising answer for a professional carer. Healing is important to me because of what I have myself received from God at the hands of other people. I am full of gratitude to God and to them for their share in God's work. It is because of that fact that I am eager for other people to find their way to the best kind of help, whether they are looking for a cure or for wholeness. So let's see if there are some guidelines that might help you to find what you're looking for, whether it be healing for yourself and others or becoming someone who assists God as an agent of healing.

CHAPTER SIX

Getting in Touch with Our Need

I was referred to a consultant who made me feel like a
rational human being.

Grace Sheppard[1]

When she was twenty-two years old Grace Sheppard
collapsed in Holborn Underground station. Her heart
was pounding, she was gasping for breath and she felt as if she
was dying. She found herself in the grip of panic: 'I was terrified. I
had come to the end of my own resources.'[2] She received some
emergency medical care before managing to get to the safety of
her own home. Grace was eventually referred to the London
Hospital for investigation. There it was decided that she had
developed agoraphobia, an acute fear of open spaces.

Grace was referred to a psychiatrist. It was he who made her
feel like a rational human being. In her book, *An Aspect of Fear*,
Grace tells of her thirty-year struggle to overcome this terrible
condition. In it she pays tribute to the professional people who
helped her: her psychiatrist, her clinical psychologist and her
spiritual director. In the preface she writes:

> Facing fear squarely and with professional help, I discovered
> how to manage it. Now, nearly thirty years later, I have,
> through a combination of factors, found a wholeness that is
> distinct from the independent perfection I had been seeking
> before. These factors included patient love from my family and
> friends, a willingness to be helped by professionals, a belief that
> God was in it all somewhere, and sheer determination to find a
> way through. It is a wholeness that I have to go on seeking.[3]

Grace Sheppard found the right help very quickly. She was
fortunate, but it was not just a matter of being in the right place

at the right time. Grace played her part in her own healing too. In her book she speaks about her consternation when her consultant suggested that she needed a spell as an in-patient in a psychiatric unit in London. She says:

> I sobbed like a child as I came to accept the reality that I needed more help. It was a letting go, and the beginning of a long climb back towards wholeness. But I did not realise this then; the shame of it took a long time to overcome.[4]

There are, I think, three elements in all true healing: knowing one's need, finding the right help, and accepting that help with the right disposition. Grace Sheppard took time to know her need; she found the right help; and she accepted that help with 'sheer determination to find a way through'. It may sound easy, but it isn't.

Knowing One's Need

> All wish to know but none want to pay the price.
>
> Juvenal (AD 60–c130)[5]

When she was young, Anne Townsend thought she knew how she wanted to live. She decided to become a missionary doctor. She married, and she and her husband worked in Thailand for a number of years. She worked extremely hard. She had a 'need' to do so. It accorded with her idea of how a missionary doctor ought to live for Christ, and for those whom she served.

When she and her family returned to England Anne went on over-working. Beneath the veneer of cheerfulness she was becoming depressed. She did not recognise her need. Then one night she felt so dreadful that she tried to commit suicide by slashing her wrists. It was not a premeditated act and when she woke in the morning to find that the weight of her body had staunched the wounds she decided to seek help.

Anne spent the next four or five years finding out what her true needs were and what she really wanted to do with her life. In the process she had to let go of a lot of her former beliefs and ways of behaving. She discovered her real self, 'and it's there you find God and it's rich, beautiful, true and somehow you can trust it.'[6]

Anne's life changed. She stopped being a doctor, 'rushing around giving medicine, suggesting treatments, even suggesting ways of getting to heaven.'[7] She started being a Christian healer by being with people in their suffering, 'not to run away, but to be there with them sharing it.'[8] Today Anne is an assistant chaplain at a London teaching hospital. She works mainly with cancer patients.

Anne Townsend's story is important because so often illness is the means by which we come to know our true needs. We have to distinguish these from the false needs we manufacture for ourselves. Anne broke down before she discovered what she really needed. She was fortunate indeed, for she might have died without making that vital discovery.

If you are ill for any length of time, and particularly if your symptoms baffle your doctors and therapists, it is worth looking at your needs. Do you need the prayer of faith instead of, or as well as, some tablets? Do you need to change your lifestyle? Do you need to mend an unhappy relationship which is affecting your health? If you have a backache, for instance, do you simply need a few pills to put it right, or a new mattress on your bed? Or are you standing badly? Or could it be that chronic unhappiness is contributing to your physical symptoms? You will only know where to look for help if you begin to recognise your needs. No one else knows you quite as well as you know yourself so it's probably up to you to do this. I should add that I often find close friends invaluable in helping me to recognise my own needs, even though I sometimes resist their effors to tell me the truth. We can be remarkably obtuse about ourselves.

'You need to relax,' someone said to me recently.

'I am relaxed,' I said rather huffily.

My tone of voice told me that I wasn't. So I went off to do some relaxation exercises. That works for me; but other people might prefer a body massage, a sauna, a good game of squash, transcendental meditation or bio-feedback. What matters is to find out what suits you. Relatives and friends do sometimes know us better than we know ourselves and we do well to listen to them, or so I try to tell myself when I'm being particularly awkward.

If you identify a need, or realise that you need some assistance on your journey towards wholeness, it often helps to tell yourself that your need may only be temporary. People sometimes run into all sorts of problems because they don't realise that what they need today they may not need at all tomorrow. I have, for instance, known people remain in psychotherapy for far too long, because they haven't recognised that they no longer have the problems which brought them for treatment in the first place.

Looking for the Right Help

No one is so rich that he does not need another's help; no one so poor as not to be useful in some way to his fellow man; and the disposition to ask assistance from others with confidence, and to grant it with kindness, is part of our very nature.

Pope Leo XIII (1810–1903)[9]

Once you have identified your immediate needs you can begin to look for the right help. I usually start by consulting my local doctor. I might also take advice from trusted friends. I investigate the healing agencies I'm going to, as far as I can. If what I'm trying doesn't seem to be helping, and I've given it a reasonable length of time, I'm prepared to change my mind. I try to keep my eyes fixed on God, whatever is happening. All that has stood me in good stead, but then I'm very fortunate. As a doctor of medicine it isn't difficult to consult other doctors; as a deacon I know my way around the Christian healing ministry. It's not nearly so easy for other people. So how do you go about it, and what guidelines can you follow?

Most people who fall ill first wait to see if the symptoms will go away by themselves. If they don't, or if they seem severe, they consult their local doctor. The next step on the healing journey is rather more difficult.

Orthodox medicine doesn't necessarily have all the right answers in one doctor's surgery. Even the most defensive doctor will admit that. In a country like Britain, where health care provision is by and large excellent, there is still plenty of room for improvement. The more you know about what scientific medicine *can* do, the more dissatisfied you tend to be with its shortcomings. You also start to question its exclusive emphasis on the preservation of life.

'Life at any cost' is not what most people want these days. they also want quality of life; in other words they want to enjoy their lives. For example I have a relative by marriage whose kidneys failed some years ago. He would have been dead long since but for renal dialysis. When you are tied down to visiting hospital three times a week for dialysis the quality of your life isn't very good. For all sorts of reasons (mainly technical) he had a long wait, but eventually he received a kidney from a living donor, his sister.

It was a good match. He was at last freed from his frequent hospital visits. He could travel, which he had always wanted to do, and he did. I think he was right to want the quality of his life to be improved. I am thankful both for the gift he received from his sister and for the knowledge and skills that made his transplant successful. Even if it ultimately fails he will have had some precious time of freedom to look back on.

That story had a relatively happy ending, but not all of them do. Orthodox medical practitioners like myself cannot afford to be complacent because of our successes. We have to improve the quality of health care for everyone. We also have to recognise that we are part of God's healing work, but not the only vehicle of healing. Other agencies of healing matter too, and often they will be better able to meet a person's needs.

People everywhere are asking for improved health care, and if the National Health Service cannot give them what they want they are going to look elsewhere. So long as that includes looking at themselves and their lifestyle I am very much in favour of it. And there are other doctors who take the same view. In *The Greening of Medicine*, Dr Patrick Pietroni writes helpfully about some of the alternatives to orthodox health care.[10] I have used his classification under four headings and have included my own brief notes on some of the more important alternatives currently on offer. I have listed the most common uses of each one, but that does not mean they are the only uses. You would need to find out more about each treatment or therapy before trying it. These notes are only intended to help you decide whether or not to make further enquiries.

1) Alternative Complete Systems of Healing

These offer diagnosis, investigative techniques and treatment.

Acupuncture and Acupressure A traditional Chinese system of medicine. The use of fine needles is described in *A Classic of Internal Medicine*, written some time between 475 and 221 BC. The internal organs are thought to be related to the surface of the body, so channels of healing to the organs can be opened up by careful placement of needles on the skin. There are 365 acupuncture points distributed over the body. **Acupressure** uses the same points but applies pressure rather than needles.

Widely used by Western practitioners in treatment of pain. Helpful in arthritis, muscular pain, headaches, migraine, neuralgia, and for anaesthesia. Also for asthma and for those who want to stop smoking.

Ayurvedic Medicine Ancient Hindu system of healing based on natural and homeopathic remedies. Uses mental techniques to alter bodily responses to disease processes, and concentration on primordial sounds, such as meaningless syllabic sounds, or mantras, to focus attention away from pain.

Popular with transcendental meditators for general improvement of well-being.

Chiropractic Introduced by an American, Daniel David Palmer, in 1895. Disease considered to be due to neural malfunction; manipulation of the spinal column and other bodily structures is preferred method of treatment.

Specially useful for arthritis, and muscle, joint and disc problems; also used for respiratory and digestive disorders.

Herbal Medicine Dates from very ancient times. Takes a holistic approach and uses natural herbal remedies.

Widely used for a variety of ailments, such as asthma, bronchitis, digestive troubles, migraine, heart conditions, urinary infections and hormonal problems.

Homeopathic Medicine Based on the principle of treating like with like. For instance, if a remedy causes an itchy rash it would be used in minute quantites to treat a similar rash, thus giving the body a chance to increase its resistance and produce a natural cure. Used for all conditions.

Osteopathy Founded by an American doctor, Andrew Taylor Still, in 1874. Disease thought to be due to interference with blood supply to organs (rather than neural malfunction, as in chiropractic). Manipulation of spine and bodily structures is main method of treatment. Drugs and surgery also used in USA, but not in Britain. Widely used for musculo-skeletal disorders, arthritis and relief of tension.

2) Alternative Diagnostic Methods
Pietroni lists a number of these alternative methods of diagnosis, some of which, like iridology, have been reliably investigated and found wanting. I have not listed them.

Kinesiology A technique developed by a chiropractor. Studies locomotion by testing relative muscle strength to find and treat weak muscles. Can sometimes localise a particular spinal problem. Used by chiropractors and others.

Psychic Diagnostic Methods Pietroni lists hair analysis and aura diagnosis among these. Blood analysis by radionics (which uses a free swinging pendulum) also comes under this heading, as does diagnostic touch.

These techniques sometimes work, but are unreliable on their own. Widely used for absent healing.

3) *Alternative Treatments*

These treatments, which include a very wide variety of touching therapies, assume that the diagnosis has already been made, either by doctors, or by alternative practitioners. They do not replace complete systems of healing but complement or supplement them. I have not included treatments like hydrotherapy (exercises in warm water) because they are available through the National Health Service.

Alexander Technique Treatment by attention to postural faults. It involves the eradication of bad habits, re-education and the cultivation of self-awareness and personal development.

Widely used by performing artists, and also seen as helpful by chiropractors and osteopaths. Gives improved sense of well-being.

Aromatherapy Massage using essential oils with specific healing properties. Known since time of Ancient Egyptians.

Widely used for chronic muscular pain and physical and emotional stress.

Massage A large variety of techniques, mainly used for soothing musculo-skeletal disorders, and for relief of stress.

Reflexology Foot and hand massage based on the theory that different parts of the body are related to different parts of the feet. Widely used for muscular disorders and general relaxation, but also for some hormonal imbalances.

Rolfing Named after Ida Rolf, a form of massage which involves deep knuckling. Quite painful, but can be very effective in relieving muscle pain and stress conditions.

Whole body massage A wide variety of techniques used for all musculo-skeletal problems and for relief of tension.

Touch therapies and spiritual healing There are references to this in Chapters Three, Five and Eight of this book, and some addresses on p. 152.

4) Self-help Measures

There are many techniques which people have to carry out for themselves. Some of them, like transcendental meditation, have to be taught. Others, like elimination diets for behavioural disorders in children (involving careful elimination of food additives and colorants), obesity diets and long fasts, need expert help which is available from the National Health Service and so they are not listed here.

Diets There are thousands of diets that are safe to try out for yourself. In general all of us who live in affluent countries can benefit from a reduction in animal fats, moderation in the use of salt and alcohol, and an increased intake of dietary fibre. The fact that there are so many diet books suggests that most of us need the encouragement of novelty to help us stick to a diet, even if we know it's good for us.

Exercise Routines Again, there are thousands to choose from. Exercise is beneficial to almost everyone, though you should consult your doctor if you want to try out some of the most energetic ones like aerobics.

    Yoga is a system of exercises which increases control over mind and body. Focus is directed towards posture, breathing and meditation. The exercises are designed to lead to better physical health and to greater self-confidence and serenity as stress and tension are reduced. It is enjoyed by large numbers of people.

Relaxation Techniques These are widely taught at Christian healing centres. They are very helpful to those of us who are prone to stress.

    Transcendental Meditation This is discussed in Chapter Three.

Visualisation A way of treating diseased areas by mentally visualising them, isolating them and overcoming them through the strength of mind over body.

Used in some cancer centres. A complementary form of treatment, not a substitute for overall care.

Even with guidance, finding the right help may take quite a while. Knowing that you have found it requires a combination of intuition and proof. People and therapies need to match. When they do, people's health often improves, but even when their health doesn't improve they often grow into a kind of serenity which bears fruit in their quality of life and ability to communicate with others. If you need further help in finding out what treatment you need you may like to contact some of the advisory centres and healing centres listed on p. 153.

In the final analysis, it will be your decision, so you will need to gather as much information as possible before approaching the person or agency you feel will meet your particular needs.

However, our responsibility does not end with our choosing a method of treatment. I often hear people saying, 'Oh, I'd trust him (or her) with my life', meaning that they have great confidence in the doctor or healing person or agency. It is good to be able to trust the person or agency we are consulting, but it is also necessary to remember that we are literally entrusting our lives to them. We have a duty to ourselves and our families to make sure that our trust is not misplaced.

From time to time we all need to stand back and ask ourselves whether what we are being told to do is reasonable and sensible and right for us. If, for instance, someone told me that I should refuse surgery for a breast lump because they could cure it with diet, deep relaxation and visualisation, I would want to ask myself, and them, some pretty searching questions before I decided to leave my own doctor's care and transfer to the traditional healer. Firstly I would ask myself whether I needed a surgical biopsy to find out exactly what it was that needed treatment. I would also ask both my own doctor and the alternative therapist how their respective treatments worked and what kind of evidence they had that their treatments did work. If, on the other hand, an Ayurvedic practitioner such as Dr Deepak Chopra, or a reputable agency such as the Bristol Cancer Centre, told me that dietary treatment, relaxation therapy and visualisation might reinforce the treatment being offered by my doctors for my proven cancer of the breast, I would be happier about accepting their help. Even then, however, I would still go on asking questions of both agencies. Ideally I would like both the orthodox and alternative practitioners to be in dialogue with each other about my care, however confident I felt about the quality of their individual services.

The situation I have described is hypothetical but in real life it is not so simple. People seem to lose their nerve, and sometimes their common sense, when it comes to asking questions of busy people who carry a great deal of authority by reason of their learning and expertise. Increasingly, however, consumers are realising that they have a right to information and they are therefore getting more. Both orthodox and alternative systems of medicine will benefit from this greater co-operation between consumers and suppliers of health care.

I shall refer again to the importance of our role in promoting good medical practice. In the meantime I want to look at how we as patients can help ourselves by the way in which we accept help from experts and other people.

Accepting Help with the Right Disposition

I have learned to be content with whatever I have. I know what it is to have little, and I know what it is to have plenty. In any and all circumstances I have learned the secret of being well-fed and of going hungry, of having plenty and of being in need. I can do all things through him who strengthens me. In any case it was kind of you to share my distress.[11]

When Grace Sheppard was ill with agoraphobia she found the strength to fight her terrible fears because she wanted to get well, not only for herself but also for her husband and daughter's sake.

When Anne Townsend revealed her condition to her conscious self by slashing her wrists she was making a desperate cry for help. It cannot have been at all easy for a doctor of medicine, who was used to being the person who always helped others, to accept help herself. She too seems to have had the motivation to face the inevitable psychological pain that curative psychotherapy entails, at any rate for a time.

Jennifer Rees Larcombe was honest enough to admit that she had become used to being ill. When God said that she would be healed she was quite resistant to the idea at first. She had begun to depend on her disability pension; she was able to help other disabled people; she was writing books; she had a full life. 'Being healed would be difficult,' she said.[12] Indeed, as she acknowledges, it *has* been difficult. In the end Jennifer also found the right disposition but not without a struggle.

What is this right disposition? Is it just a matter of an individual's determination and strength of will? Is it a matter of absolute faith in God? Do you have to want to be well in order to be healed? Some of the most perceptive reflections I have found on those kinds of questions come from the pen of the Very Reverend Michael Mayne, Dean of Westminster Abbey.

Michael Mayne was Vicar of Great St Mary's Church, Cambridge, when he fell ill with a prolonged and debilitating illness, which was finally diagnosed as myalic encephalomyelitis. This illness (which is sometimes called post-viral syndrome because it often follows a viral infection) produces symptoms such as muscular pain and weakness, and exhaustion; together with mental problems such as confusion, loss of memory and lapses of concentration. It is not easy to diagnose, and some doctors do not even recognise it as a disease. People with this condition have to be very patient, for it tends to go into spontaneous remission and then just as suddenly precipitates its victim into a relapse. This means that just as you think you are getting better, you find yourself feeling very ill again. You may feel you are back to where you started. You may lose your confidence. It is a very difficult illness to put up with, not only for the sufferers but also for their families and colleagues.

Michael Mayne had determination, courage and a loving family. During his illness he was approached about becoming Dean of Westminster Abbey. He wasn't at all sure that he could do it, but he wanted the job. The motivation to get well was there and he had all the right help, but for a long while his condition fluctuated. Towards the end of the most disabling year of his life, when he was slowly recovering, he recorded his experiences in a book called *A Year Lost and Found*[13]

It is interesting to find that he did what I have advocated. He shopped around. He consulted several orthodox doctors, an acupuncturist, and a holistic doctor who prescribed massage and dietary treatment. He received help from his family, his friends, his fellow priests and a retired bishop. He slowly gained insight into his illness and into himself. He also found out what it was like to be on the receiving end of pastoral care and discovered how important it was to note what helped him and what didn't. For instance, he speaks very highly of touch as a therapy, and says of illness:

> You *do* feel cut off and you do need reassuring. And the best and most effective way of achieving both is by touch and by prayer. I was so grateful to the small number of priests who overcame their understandable shyness with a fellow priest and laid hands on me and blessed me; and I knew which way I should decide in future when visiting sick people either at home or in hospital.[14]

Michael Mayne also details three important insights which he acquired during his illness. The first was that his body had the power to renew itself, against all his gloomy expectations. The second was that his 'inscape' or inner landscape ('those truths I seek to live by, speak about, hold important') hadn't matched his 'landscape', the actual bit of the world where he functioned; and that mismatch had contributed to his illness. The third insight was that he wanted to learn the lessons of his illness so that his 'lost year' could become a valued part of his life journey.

He did learn those lessons and was able to move on to Westminster Abbey with conviction and confidence, even though when he took up his post he had still not fully recovered from his illness. He is still improving.

Knowing the strength of Michael's faith and determination, as I do, his book told me a great deal about how to find the right disposition to accept help. It seems that one of the most important aspects of illness is learning its lessons. When we recover or partially recover, or slowly move towards accepting chronic disability or death, having learnt those lessons will give us the right disposition for the wholeness that God wants us to find. We shall not become whole during our lifetimes, but we shall at least glimpse what it is we are moving towards.

The answers to the questions posed by suffering will vary for each of us. Other people's stories often touch our own at some point, and Michael's remarks about his inscape not matching his landscape certainly found a deep echo in my life at a time when I needed to hear them. Therein lies the value of listening to the experiences of our relatives and friends, and people whose acquaintance we make through books, when we ourselves are living through a difficult part of our journey towards wholeness. When illness has struck in my own life I have often had to ask myself many of these same questions, and I have also referred to other people's responses to them. However ultimately it isn't other people's success stories that matter but our own struggles, successes and failures.

It is all very well to talk about looking for the help we need, but what if we don't find it, or we do find it and yet everything seems to go wrong? What about unrelieved suffering? What about the ghastly mistakes made by doctors and other caring professionals? What about times when God appears to be absent? What about 'the valley of the shadow of death'? I do not think there *are* any answers to these questions, but there is a way of living with them; one I would like to share.

CHAPTER SEVEN

When Things Go Wrong

The deeper the sorrow, the less tongue it has.

Jewish saying[1]

Many years ago I looked after a woman who had multiple sclerosis. I will call her Dorothy. She was severely disabled. She lived in a wheelchair by day and had to be lifted in and out of her bed at night. She had extensive pressure sores and bladder problems. She had impaired eyesight. She had no religious faith. She was dying.

A characteristic of multiple sclerosis is that many of its victims seem to display a particular cheerfulness in the face of progressive deterioration. Dorothy showed a remarkably brave face to the world. Her husband, John, tried to keep up with her, but he suffered greatly, especially as he did not have the same kind of emotional protection.

John had given up his job some years before I knew them. They were living on her disability allowance and his social security benefit. Life was not easy. John did everything for his wife and scarcely ever left her alone. From time to time I and the district nurses would suggest that Dorothy went into hospital for a few days so that John could have a much-needed break. She couldn't bring herself to do that, and he never encouraged her, so in all the ten years I knew them she only went away once.

In the face of this unrelieved suffering John's personality changed. Whereas previously he had been patient and kind, he became impatient and unkind. Whereas previously he had been grateful to members of the caring professions for the help they gave his wife, he now became querulous and critical. He was plainly exhausted, yet he could not give up his self-services are used to such things happening, and those who minister at such services are there to see that people do not hurt themselves.

I have attended many such services. I have been moved to see what happens, but I have never been 'caught up' in what is going on. Yet I feel sure that I too receive the gifts the Holy Spirit means me to have. I would hope that if you are someone who has been 'slain in the Spirit', or suddenly moved to speak in tongues, or found yourself shaking all over – all of which do happen to many people during certain kinds of healing services – you would accept that my experience was as genuine a contact with the Holy Spirit as yours. The Holy Spirit can come suddenly and swiftly, or slowly and more gently, in the still silence at the centre of one's being. It is God's choice as to how God comes to us. It is our choice as to how we respond.

Up to now I have been talking about activities which are part of Christian experience, but which don't require church membership. Anyone can pray, including agnostics and atheists who are often surprised to find themselves doing so. To make use of the Christian sacraments of healing, however, implies that one is a member of a Trinitarian church. Some devoutly religious people do not have any sacraments; that is they do not use outward signs like water, bread and wine to express an inward reality. It is not the way of either the Quakers or the Salvation Army, for instance. Quakers feel that the whole of life is a sacrament and so they have no need of any symbolic contact with God through Baptism or the Eucharist. Salvationists place more emphasis on personal conversion than on water Baptism or the Eucharist, though in my experience they are happy to share in Communion with other Christians and to take part in healing services and individual ministry to the sick. For those who do use the sacraments, how do they fit into healing?

Healing Sacraments

A sacrament is 'an outward and visible sign of an inward and spiritual grace', as the 1662 *Book of Common Prayer* tells us.[16]

appointed task. Instead of accepting the help that was offered, he berated all carers for their failure to find a cure for Dorothy's condition and for their failure to relieve her symptoms. It was a sad situation. We who belonged to the team of carers began to dread our visits. We were saddened by what was happening, and our frustration at being unable to help either of them added to our pain. In the end all that I and the other caring professionals could hope for was that Dorothy would die quickly and in comparative comfort. I can remember praying for this to happen for a year or two before she died and being angry with God that it didn't happen as I wanted it to happen!

When at last Dorothy did die, John was relieved and desolate at one and the same time. However he made a remarkably swift recovery from his bereavement, and his personality returned to its former pleasant self. I was relieved, but also troubled. I wondered what would have happened to John if Dorothy had not died when she did. I wondered why he had found it so difficult to allow himself a break from time to time. He had told me that what had made a difference to him was that he had been satisfied that he had done his best, even when it seemed that he was going under and I was urging him to allow other people to care for Dorothy. It had preserved his self-respect. I saw his point of view, but I wondered whether he was right. Surely a few days rest would have made him more able to manage a dreadful situation. Should I have put more pressure on him?

The point of this story is that when such disastrous illnesses occur there are no right or wrong solutions to our problems. I'm not sure that John found the best solution. It did seem to help his self-esteem, but the cost – both to himself and others – was high. I still think he would have benefited from accepting help. But in the end the choice had to be his. For him, its rightness must have outweighed its disadvantages. Yet in a different kind of family John's brand of stubbornness might have been disastrous. I have known of a similar situation where a devoted wife cared for her bedridden husband for years on end. One day she could bear it no longer. Something inside her snapped. She simply walked out of the house, and never came back. Her poor husband was devastated and ended his life in hospital. Her children were grown up, but very upset. As for her, I don't know. It must have been a terrible decision to make.

Dorothy and John's situation gave me much to think about. What do we do when disaster strikes? How do we cope? How do we manage to live through the experience? How dare we talk of healing when it is so obvious that the longed-for cure is not going to come? How do we relate to God? Is it really any help to think of Jesus being there with us in our suffering? These are all questions which crowd in on us, and I think the answers very much depend on the kind of disaster that strikes our lives, and the point at which it makes its initial impact.

I tend to divide disasters into four categories. Firstly, there are disasters that I call natural and understandable, such as the death of a much-loved parent who has lived a long and good life. Secondly, there are those that are unnatural but understandable – the kind of thing that happens when someone has a heart attack at the wheel of their car. The driver loses control of the car which swerves across the road and kills a child. The death is cruel enough but at least the bereaved relatives know that there are mitigating circumstances. Thirdly, there are the terrible things that need never happen at all: the kind of disaster that is due to medical negligence; or that happens because a drunken man drives a car, when everyone around him knows he shouldn't but doesn't have the courage to stop him. This kind of disaster might also happen when an innocent bystander is killed in a gun battle between criminals; or a bomb kills, or permanently disables, an adult or child. These are man-made disasters. They seem to most of us both cruel and senseless. It feels as if innocent lives have been cut short by the irresponsible or criminal actions of other human beings.

Fourthly, there are the disasters that seem to me to be 'perverse acts of God'. These are the disasters that are definitely not man-made. They too are apparently unjust and cruel. They have no explanation and seem so often to strike the good and the innocent. Among these I include cot deaths, the births of genetically handicapped children, and deaths from floods, tidal waves, hurricanes, earthquakes, volcanic eruptions, lightning, drought and spontaneous fires.

Natural Disasters

Dorothy's death comes into the first of these groups. It was both natural and understandable. Disease and death are part of life. In that sense they are natural. Most of us suffer from some severe illness during our lifetimes. We do not expect to be spared all suffering. We may ask 'Why me?' at the beginning of any life-threatening illness, but most of us will come to terms with being seriously ill. Once we have done that, we are freed to find our healing in and through it. Dorothy went through all the normal stages of grief at the gradual loss of her mobility – denial, anger, depression and finally acceptance. Both she and John used anger to help them feel that they had some control over their lives. Admittedly, it might have been unpleasant for those who were on the receiving end of their anger, but I do not think that mattered very much. It is, after all, the task of a caring team to understand and accept, rather than to be critical.

It is comparatively easy to move towards healing in the kind of natural disasters I have been describing. The disaster is concrete. You have something to hold on to. There are all kinds of things that both the suffering victim and his or her relatives and friends can do in terms of relieving suffering. It is not just a matter of good nursing, skilful pain control and alleviation of fear. There are also the small kindnesses and thoughtful actions that mean so much when one is ill, whether or not one is going to get well. Quite tiny things can make an enormous difference: actions such as putting a glass of water in reach, moving a glaring light away, sitting still and quiet and holding a person's hands. These are the kinds of things that say we love someone enough to anticipate their needs and to hold them tenderly.

110

One of the most important ways of bringing healing to a family afflicted by natural and understandable disaster is to help the sick person and his or her caring relatives to communicate effectively. If individuals within a family can share their feelings and fears it makes a tremendous difference to everyone, especially, I think, to the relatives. If and when death comes to such a family, each member knows that they have had time to say what they needed to say to the person who had died. I have certainly seen old hurts healed, old sins forgiven, old and cruel memories dissolved by such openness in families where one member is suffering or dying.

Sometimes, however, there is no direct sharing of grief. In some families there is a sense of despair because, however much they may want it to, the sharing never happens. Fear of an emotional scene, or fear of making the dying person feel worse, stops the family from talking directly about anything that is important. This doesn't really matter as long as the people concerned can recognise what is happening. Just like people who cannot speak the same language, so two or more people who cannot say what they want to say may need an interpreter.

One of my most precious memories is of being with a mother when she was dying. She had been estranged from her husband for many years. He came to see her when she was near the end of her life and was very upset to find her in pain. He felt that talking about the past would open old wounds, and she had begged me not to say anything to him about her own pain. So I sat down with him and listened to his story. I heard about his own pain, but also about his desire to tell his wife how sorry he was for some of the things he had said and done to her. He could tell me because I was outside their mutual pain. With his permission I relayed some of what he had said to his wife at a time when she was able to hear it; again, being a trusted person helped.

When he next came, the atmosphere in the room was very different. Nothing was said. There was just a warm embrace, a few tears, some silence and unspoken recognition of forgiveness on both sides. I know that to be true because they were my parents and both of them spoke independently to me about that moment. I was their go-between.

It is unusual, perhaps, for a daughter to be able to act in that way for her parents, but as an outsider I have been able to do something similar for other people. It also seems to me that through prayer we can even be reconciled to relatives, friends and enemies who are dead. Such actions can be very healing, irrespective of the outcome of the illness.

Unnatural but Understandable Disasters

James broke his neck in a diving accident. He had left home that morning full of excitement, having just passed his university entrance examination. Two hours later he was on his way to hospital with a broken neck and paralysed arms and legs. Two days later his parents were told that he would never walk again. Two years later James went to university in his wheelchair. Twenty years later he is still alive, still wheelchair-bound. He is one of the most whole people I know.

There was no one to blame for the accident but James himself. His parents never said that to him. He said it to himself. He said it many times in the first few weeks when he was flat on his back in a hospital bed. There was a stage, a few months into his paralysis, when James felt so negative about his future that he became apathetic and unco-operative about his physiotherapy. He felt that he wanted to be left to drift into death. He might have gone under, but he had supportive parents and a marvellous team of doctors and nurses. They encouraged him, bullied him, teased him, angered him and evoked in him a desire to live. He gradually recovered his sense of humour and it stood him in good stead during the long weary months of readjustment to his new situation. He made that adjustment and in the course of learning to live in a new way he helped many others with similar problems.

When people have to face either a natural disaster, or an unnatural one which is understandable, they often gain profound insights into the nature of their disabilities, and end up using their energies for the benefit of people like themselves. One thinks immediately of Jack Ashley MP, who has done so much for those who are handicapped by deafness, and of Lady Masham who contributed so greatly to the foundation of the Disability Alliance.

Doctors like myself are very aware of the work done by Timothy (Timbo) and his mother, Elizabeth Ward.[2] Timothy was thirteen years old when he developed acute nephritis. Four years later his renal failure was so severe that he had to be treated by renal dialysis. He had three transplants, the last a gift from his father. All eventually failed. In 1975 he and his mother founded the British Kidney Patient Association which has been instrumental in raising the morale and hopes of many kidney failure patients.

One thinks also of people like Christy Nolan,[3] the poet who has cerebral palsy and who tells us what being handicapped feels like. Writers like Mary Craig,[4] Frances Young[5] and Margaret Spufford[6] also come to mind. Their openness about their struggles to care for mentally and physically handicapped children in a relatively uncaring society, has contributed to the development of better services for such children. But there are countless other people, like James, whose names are not so well known, who have used their wounds to bring healing to other wounded people like themselves.

James, for instance, has worked untiringly for paraplegics. He knows what it is like. He is articulate. He has used his energy for the benefit of people like himself. He still goes to see new paraplegics who are brought into his local hospital. He has a remarkable way of being able to give hope to people who are newly paralysed without making them feel that he is so wonderful that they will never be able to emulate him. He is a rich source of healing within that hospital. There are many like him in other parts of the country and in different circumstances.

People like Christy Nolan and James are incurable in the ordinary sense of the word. They have to face disasters which the majority of us will never have to face. In their struggles to

113

retain their human dignity and to relate to the rest of us in creative ways they bring blessing not only to themselves and to people like them, but also to many apparently well and healthy people with whom they come into contact.

The people whose sufferings I have so far described in this chapter – Dorothy, James, Timbo, Jack Ashley, Christy Nolan and the three mothers with severely handicapped children – had to come to terms with obviously incurable diseases. Either their illnesses were progressive or their disabilities were visible and permanent. There is a sense in which they knew what they had to face, but there is another group of people for whom I think the suffering is equally great. These are the men, women and children who ought to get better, or could recover, but don't. They are the people whose illnesses fluctuate in intensity, or whose sufferings become chronic and yet largely invisible to other people. They are well represented by Jane Grayshon.

In 1976, Jane Grayshon, at that time an enthusiastic and energetic professional nurse married to an Anglican ordinand, had an inflamed appendix removed. The operation went well. She should have made a complete recovery, as thousands of people do every year. Instead, she developed an abscess. The surgeons operated again and when they looked inside her abdominal cavity they found it full of pus. They gave her all the right treatment and again Jane should have made a good recovery, but she didn't. She developed adhesions, tough bands of inflammatory fibrous tissue, which tethered her intestines to themselves, to other organs and to the lining of the abdominal cavity.

In normal healthy people the intestines can slide about inside us and we are quite unaware of their movements except when we get an urge to defaecate or suffer from occasional colic or 'wind'. When there are adhesions, however, the intestines cannot slide about so easily. They often hurt because of this and they also sometimes get inflamed again. Sometimes loops of bowel get 'hung up' or twisted around an adhesion. The intestines can then become distended and obstructed.

All these things have happened to Jane. Three or four times a year she has found herself in hospital for treatment of severe episodes of pain, and she has had several exploratory operations to see what can be done to help her. Unfortunately such operations sometimes result in more adhesions. In Jane's case it seems that the disease process spread to other organs in the abdomen for she had to have a hysterectomy when she was still young enough to have children of her own.

In her book, *A Pathway through Pain*,[7] Jane describes the effects of her fluctuating fortunes on herself and her family during these long years of illness. Her suffering has been very real. Some of it has come from her physical symptoms. Some of it has come from the fact that she sometimes looks quite well even when she is in severe pain, and so people do not find it easy to understand that her suffering is real. She dreads being thought to be exaggerating her symptoms in order to gain attention or pity so she tends to drag herself around for far longer than she ought to. Moreover, as is so often the case, her professional advisers have sometimes disagreed about the best way of helping her, and this has added to her mental and spiritual anguish and confusion.

Jane has met her illness with great courage. She has managed to remain a nurse. She and her husband Matthew have adopted two children. They have fought her illness with determination. They have had the help of good professional advisers and caring pastors. Although she has had a considerable struggle to retain her faith she has done so.

In her book Jane pays tribute to her Christian friends and pastors. One section which I found especially moving describes a time when she felt that she had come to the end of her tether. After a particularly unpleasant spell in hospital she went to stay with a friend called Tina who was one of her husband's college lecturers. One night Tina found Jane clutching a bottle of pills. It had seemed that she could not endure the pain any longer. Jane could not understand why God did not seem to be helping her. Tina's sensitive compassion and quiet silence in the face of the mystery of such anguish enabled Jane to go on asking her questions of God. Eventually Tina shared some of her own experience of suffering with Jane, without attempting to give logical answers to the mystery of suffering. Jane writes of that encounter:

> In these moments of loving sympathy Tina, almost unwittingly, was leading me towards a most important and health-giving insight. I – a fighter by nature – began to see that God wanted to give me the strength not to fight against his will but to embrace it. I thus began to understand one of the essential secrets within the mystery of suffering.[8]

It is important, I think, to understand that God does not will our pain. Suffering is not sent as a kind of punishment or test to see how much we can stand. People like Jane Grayshon do, however, believe that even when they can't see or feel God, God is there with them; that when inescapable suffering comes to any of us God offers us the help that will enable us to accept, endure and be transformed by the experience. From her own experience of this mystery Jane says:

> To some extent joy grows out of suffering. To ask for the fruit of the Holy Spirit to be seen in my life was to accept God's hand completely. In his great wisdom he seems to have chosen to teach me his path to joy through suffering.[9]

I rejoice that this seems to have happened to Jane, but my faith has had to take me a step further because I have had to watch so many people in whom this simply does not happen. They are defeated by their pain and anguish. They are not able to face it heroically. They become embittered and distorted by it, and this applies as much to mental and spiritual pain as to physical suffering. Is God not in that too? Yes, I believe God is in that too, but I can't explain why. Nor, if I am myself plunged into that kind of hell, can I find God anywhere in myself or my own suffering. I have a kind of blind faith that it is so, that is all.

On the other hand I have noticed that such unmitigated suffering has a transforming effect on those who are outside it, yet are willing to be with the one who is suffering. The kinds of disasters I have been describing can bring out the best qualities in many people. It happened to me when my friend Kath was dying of cancer. It has happened to me with other people. And I have seen it happen to other people too.

This kind of disaster is so appalling that everyone who has anything to do with such a person and his or her family finds themselves wanting to help. People in these circumstances seem to be able to put themselves into the sufferer's shoes relatively easily. This makes it easier for them to offer the kind of help they would like to receive, were they to be in a similar situation.

It seems important to recognise that nearly all of us respond to other people's misfortunes according to an internal sliding scale. People who are blind receive more sympathy, for instance, than people who are deaf. Young people attract more help than elderly ones. Physically handicapped people generally receive better care than mentally handicapped people whom society seems to prefer to isolate. People who are paralysed by accident or misfortune of war attract more help than those who suffer from multiple sclerosis or muscular dystrophy. Yet it is also true that if a well-known person suffers from any of these conditions everyone else benefits from the publicity. David Niven's long-drawn-out suffering, for instance, helped many people who suffered from motor neurone disease. Within this sliding scale there is another important factor. So-called 'innocent' suffering seems to attract more sympathy than illnesses which are apparently one's one responsibility. It is remarkable how uncompassionate many of us can be towards alcoholics and people who have AIDS.

In a recent book about some possible Christian responses to AIDS called *Embracing the Chaos*, its editor James Woodward includes the story of Charles. He was a well-to-do American lawyer who developed the disease when he was in his mid-thirties. When he received the news he and his partner Paul, who was a Christian, were emotionally shocked but confident that their close friends, all of whom were white and affluent like themselves, would support them. Alas that didn't happen:

But when Paul telephoned to tell them the news, they suddenly fell silent, and made excuses about having to rush on to an important meeting. They never called, or visited. Sometimes Paul saw them drive past the house on their way to work. They were so busy.[10]

The two men had discovered the 'sliding scale'. It applied to their Christian minister too. In desperation they asked for help from an organisation for people with HIV infection. A black lady called Eunice came to see them, a woman from a section of their urban community they would have formerly never have gone out of their way to meet, and of whom they would have been somewhat afraid:

> It was she, and only she, who stuck with Paul through the long painful months of Charles's illness; and when the time came, she did her best to help Paul face life without Charles.[11]

Tony Chard, an Englishman, had a similar experience of some people's 'sliding scales' when he told his friends about his HIV infection, but he also had some rather happier experiences:

> I suppose that the first twelve months was the darkest period, I think I was reeling with shock and I refused help from everyone. I thought – I am going to fight this alone . . . the big change came when I plucked up courage to ask for help; that was the first step forward, that is the point when things began to change.[12]

Tony found out about the London Lighthouse, a hospice and homecare service for people with AIDS. This source of hope for many people grew out of a meeting of some concerned people in July 1989. Tony joined one of its support groups, learnt to talk about his feelings and began to develop positive attitudes towards himself. He now works for the Lighthouse. He claims he is completely different from the person he was four years ago:

I am still fairly scatty and a hectic sort of person, but now I actually have goals and ambitions which I strive to achieve . . . what is good is that I am actually achieving them, not because I think I am going to drop dead any minute but because NOW, the present, is a good time – the first year I did worry about dying and that was partly my motivation but that has changed. I find that the more I achieve the stronger I feel and the more I want to do . . .

I can say that having the virus has had its benefits . . . I do feel more at peace and in touch with myself and the world. The fear I had has passed and I can now get on and do all the things that are important. It doesn't matter if I have a matter of years, or go on to 1001.[13]

When you read stories like those of Charles and Tony, or meet people with AIDS, and their families, your value system is challenged. Your 'sliding scale', which usually operates so subtly that you are scarcely aware of its existence, is exposed and is available for careful scrutiny.

If you, like me, are aware of having that kind of attitude, it is possible to develop an awareness of the need to support people with less attractive, less 'worthy' diseases. At least that can redress some of the pain that people with less acceptable diseases have to suffer. Healing is not only for those who are ill. It is for the rest of us too, and it is important to recognise how much we who are apparently well need to be healed.

Unnatural Incomprehensible Disasters

These disasters are much harder to contend with. They are the terrible events which we find so hard to understand because they are frequently due to someone's negligence. A drunken driver kills our only son. A careless error during an operation leaves our daughter unconscious on a life-support machine. A parcel bomb blows off both our hands. A medical procedure which should have been safe leaves us crippled or paralysed. A child is physically or sexually abused and his or her innocent trust in other people is destroyed, often for life. What do we –

whether we are the person concerned, or a relative or friend –
do with that kind of suffering and how can we find healing in
that kind of disaster?

The first thing most of us do is get very angry, especially if
the person concerned denies all responsibility, or is totally
indifferent to our suffering or that of someone we love. Anger
in these circumstances is so natural that most of us tend to
think there is something wrong with someone who is instantly
forgiving. From time to time some heroic person appears on
television immediately after their relative has been killed and
affirms their forgiveness of the murderers, but most of us are
not like that except during the period of immediate shock.

Once the truth sinks in, that one is going to be in a
wheelchair for life, or disfigured, or obliged to care for a
brain-damaged relative who can never be left, the survival
instinct reasserts itself. Survival in these circumstances
depends on one's financial viability so it is not at all surprising
that people often go to law to get compensation for the negligence or other culpable offence. It is sad that this should be
necessary at all, for many countries operate a humane system
of financial recompense that does not involve prolonged and
costly legal battles. Financial compensation may help on the
practical side, but obviously nothing can replace lost health or
a lost life.

In the end people either become bitter and nurse their grief,
or they come to terms with what has happened and try to
forgive the person or people who caused the damage or loss of
life. This is no easy task and may take many, many years. If
you want to be healed, to move towards your ultimate goal of
becoming a whole human being, then that first step of forgiving someone else for a hurt done to you is essential. How
can that step be taken?

In an article in the Roman Catholic journal *Concilium*,
published in April 1986, Raymond Studzinski looks at the
psychological dimensions of forgiveness.[14] He places the initiative for forgiveness firmly with God, who alone can give us
the desire to forgive. He says that forgiveness is 'a wilful

process in which the forgiver chooses not to retaliate but rather to respond in a loving way to one who has caused the injury.'[15]

He goes on to list five conditions which have to be present if someone is to forgive: firstly, the person has to recognise his or her need to forgive; secondly, the person has to have the desire and intention to forgive; thirdly, the person has to be able to 're-member' the incident which calls for forgiveness, that is to reawaken both the memory of the incident and the emotions that accompany that memory; fourthly, the person has to accept that he or she also needs forgiving; fifthly, the person has to be willing to start a new relationship with the man or woman or institution whom they are forgiving. That does not mean that one immediately goes out and shakes hands with the rapist who has violated oneself, or one's daughter. So often, however, the hatred we feel for someone who has injured us in this or other ways is so great and lasting that it binds us to the perpetrator of the cruelty. In such circumstances we can become twisted by our own bitterness. It is letting go of that unforgiving spirit that heals us.

I believe the third condition is the hardest to fulfil. There is much pain in re-entering a memory like this. Sometimes the anticipation is worse than the pain itself, and if you are a person who dreads pain you will probably do your best to avoid going back to the memory. If that is so, then the pain is likely to fester at a subconscious level and stop you being able to forgive. To say 'I forget you' and to wipe someone out of your mind is comparatively easy. To remember and forgive is extremely difficult. Studzinski says:

> What prompts forgiveness is an injury which is held in the memory in such a way that it returns to consciousness to re-inflict its pain.[16]

To find that pathway, to allow that memory to surface is an act of great courage. It is something that I would want someone's help to do: I would not be ashamed to ask a friend or a wise counsellor to sit with me while I reclaimed that half-buried, half-forgotten memory. Some people may need the help of a psychiatrist or psychotherapist. These trained people are well qualified to help where there are deep-seated emotional problems, and people should turn to them more often than they do.

It may take a long time before you can face the emotions associated with that incident. You may think you have forgiven and find that you haven't. You will only know that you have succeeded when the memory can be recalled without its usual associated negative emotions, such as a thirst for retribution. When that happens there is a deep sense of peace and you know that you have let it go for ever.

Forgiving is an internal act. It can sometimes be accompanied by an external action, such as a kiss or a handshake, but it is often impossible to meet the person who hurt you in the first place. Nevertheless the action is real and the healing is correspondingly real. When it happens it is immensely freeing and, sometimes for the first time, one begins to understand some of the mitigating factors that are there in nearly every such disaster.

Perverse Disasters

I have left to the last a group of disasters which I personally find the hardest to come to terms with, the kind of disaster which has no apparent reason, no precipitating cause, involves no human error, but which might be loosely called 'an act of God'. I am thinking mainly about the genetic disasters which cause the births of some profoundly handicapped children, but I am also talking about one of the cruellest events in anyone's life, a 'near cot death' where the child does not die but is left profoundly handicapped. The day before the event the parents had a perfectly healthy baby. The day after, he or she is left brain-damaged. It is a most terrible and totally un-understandable event. I have cared for two families in which this has happened. Each time I have felt outraged by such cruelty.

I spent seven years of my working life as a school doctor. During that time I saw many severely handicapped children and a great many bewildered parents struggling to care for their very dependent children. Initially, I felt angry indeed with God who allowed such children to be born alive, who allowed them to suffer as they did, who allowed their parents to exhaust themselves. It was only much later that both the children and their parents taught me that, while I could give very little to them, I could receive a great deal from them. I learnt that lesson the day I began to see two small boys as two individuals rather than as children with mental and physical handicaps due to the same genetic disorder.

Their mother brought them in for their end-of-term check-up. Daniel was nine years old, David, seven. Neither could walk or talk or feed themselves. Both had severe learning difficulties. Both were visually handicapped and one was deaf. I had seen each boy several times in their school classroom, but as they were in separate classes I had never before seen them together. Seeing them that day with their mother in the same room I saw them quite differently. Their reactions were different from each other and so their individual characters showed through their common handicaps. Each boy was obviously loved by his mother but in different ways. She knew them as her sons. I had previously thought more about their appalling handicaps than about them as children. She knew what their likes and dislikes were, and how to get the very best out of them. So did their teachers. I did not.

As I sat there it felt as if I was seeing those two children for the first time. I also realised that I had been afraid of their handicaps because they made me angry with God, and that was unacceptable to me at the time. As soon as I saw the boys and their mother as people like myself I stopped thinking of their handicaps and started to think of their potential.

That meeting made a difference to the way I worked during the next six years of my life as a doctor. I learnt to receive from handicapped children and their parents, and that was a great grace. I learnt to draw out their potential. I became more whole myself as I watched them overcoming their fragmentation, and I learnt not to label people. Or at least I tried not to label them. I came to agree with Stanley Hauerwas and Bonita

Raine, two Americans who see the handicapped people with whom they work from a Christian perspective. In a joint essay, the fruit of their considerable experience, they say:

> From our convictions which come from deep within the Christian tradition, we have tried to suggest the fundamental concern that must be met if we are to work towards a solution – namely that we must be the kind of people who are capable of recognising the other without fear and/or resentment. If we can be this kind of community, then we may find we do not even need the label 'retarded', and that we can explore more creative ways at once to help those different from us without that help being a form of discrimination.[17]

The discovery that I could relate to God's children without fear or resentment was a breakthrough. It led me to an awareness of how they, speaking from their hearts, could touch my own. And they, living in their woundedness, could heal my wounds. I was able to stop being so angry with God and to get on with doing what I could to ensure that handicapped young people received the educational and medical services they deserved.

Faith and Disaster

It is when I am confronted with these perverse disasters that my faith is most challenged. I am aware that the God whom I continue to rage at from time to time is an image of who I think God is, rather than the reality. The God I want to relate to stands beyond my image of who I want God to be. That mysterious presence draws me into relationship as the stereotyped image cannot. Seeing that presence in handicapped people my faith in God has deepened rather than weakened.

What is the role of faith in relation to disaster? I have no answers to the problem of suffering, whatever its cause. I have no solutions for people who ask me awkward theological questions about why God permits suffering. Other people have, but I have to be honest and say that I haven't. I do not even find it possible to feel that Christ is with me when I am suffering. It doesn't feel like that at all and when people say that to me I hear them as from a great distance. They may comfort themselves but they don't comfort me. It is only *after* the suffering is over that I can see some possible meaning in it. Then I do know that I have learnt something, even if that 'something' is only that I have survived.

That is what I feel, but what I believe by faith is that God is with us at all times and in all places, nearer to us than the air we breathe, so near that we cannot see him as separate from ourselves. In good times I try to build up that faith, to lay down stores as it were against the bad times. When disaster strikes, and my capacity to survive is tested, I pray that faith (which is a link between God and myself) will hold me, even though I cannot perceive it at work.

So I continue to live in hope. I am but one of many who do so. It is St Paul who leads the way:

> In hope we were saved. Now hope that is seen is not hope. For who hopes for what is seen? But if we hope for what we do not see, we wait for it with patience.[18]

We follow. We may not always understand. We may not always feel God's presence with us, but we are aware of a mysterious call to become whole even in the midst of chaos and darkness, and we respond to that call in the strength of the Holy Spirit. The Spirit of God may be responsible for prompting us to follow, but we have a responsibility too and it is to our share in God's healing work that I now turn.

CHAPTER EIGHT

Taking Responsibility

Where falls not hail or any snow
Nor ever wind blows loudly, but it lies
Deep meadowed, happy, fair, with orchard lawns
And bowery hollows crowned with summer seas
Where I will heal me of my grievous wound.[1]

Alfred, Lord Tennyson (1819–1892)

When I first read Tennyson's words about Avalon, that idyllic island valley, I found myself soothed and healed by the very thought of such a beautiful place in which to heal my own wounds. Then, straightway, I rebelled. How could anyone heal themselves? Wasn't that God's business? Hadn't I been saying that all along? Well, yes I had, and no, I hadn't. Ambroise Paré's words, 'I bandage; God heals, are still true. Healing is a kind of co-operation between God and us. But, even after all these years of knowing my own need of healing, and of being involved in the healing ministry, I find that I still want to burden God with most of the responsibility. Even now I have to make a conscious effort to do my share of the work.

At the back of a church where I used to serve, there are candles for visitors to light. Nearby there is a notice saying that if anyone wishes to leave a prayer request in a nearby box it will be used by the whole congregation during the following Sunday's worship.

Week by week I used to take those prayers out of the box and gather them into our public prayers on the Sunday. They were very simple, very sincere. 'Please pray for my Gran who's in hospital,' 'Please God make John better,' 'Pray that my daughter gets a job soon': many prayers like that, and a few 'thank yous' too. It was, and is, very touching to see people pouring their hearts out to God and trusting that the people who put the box there will honour their promise to pray.

I still pray for all the people who use that church and that box. And I do so with sincerity, but at the same time I ask myself some questions about it. For those people, and I too, want someone outside ourselves, namely God, to do something for us that we cannot do for ourselves. We want this all-powerful figure to take our burdens away from us and give us our heart's desire.

Yes, I know my description of the feelings of those who ask for prayers and those who pray is over-simplified, and, in some instances, might be quite wrong. Nevertheless, it's how I feel and how I know some other people feel about intercession. I do want God to take responsibility. I hope that God's mind and my mind will be in tune, and that what I want God will also want.

I don't see anything wrong with this way of praying. It's certainly not childish, though it is, I think, child-like, and all the better for that. One of my colleagues in the healing ministry, Christopher Hamel Cooke, has put this experience into theological terms:

> Health is for God. We are to seek health for His sake, and
> healing as a means to that end. Health ultimately means
> holiness, the perfection of our relationship with Him. On our
> journey to that goal we encounter sickness and pain. We offer it
> to God in the spirit of the Gethsemane prayer; we ask for what
> we want, but pray that His will may be done.[2]

But the answer I get to such prayers is very often that God's will is that I should get involved in my own healing. It can't all be left to him. For one thing God seems to be mysteriously 'absent' most of the time. Speaking about silent prayer, a priest, Andrew Norman, reflects on God's silence:

> But the God we find may not be the one we want or even
> expect. In times of personal crisis, or when we stand helplessly
> beside the sufferings of others, we pray for a God who will *act*.
> But what we find, and that only if we are patient, is simply the

bruised body of his presence. We meet the One who suffers in our sufferings; in the darkness we stumble against the crucified whose passivity has mysteriously and disappointingly not yet been succeeded in the victory of the resurrection, for he still 'opens not his mouth'.[3]

Being mysteriously absent, yet present in the 'bruised body', God's passivity and identification with our sufferings invites us to share in the task of healing. We become aware that we have considerable responsibility, both for our own health and for other people's. Although I want to look at these responsibilities separately they are in fact very closely linked.

Taking Responsibility for Ourselves

They are happy who are at peace with themselves.
To begin with oneself, but not to end with oneself;
To start from oneself, but not to aim at oneself;
To comprehend oneself, but not to be preoccupied with oneself.
Martin Buber (1878–1965)[4]

Martin Buber was a Viennese Jew who was Professor of the Sociology of Religion at Jerusalem University. His best-known book, *I and Thou*, is about the relationships between human beings and objects, persons and God. His prayer comes out of his great experience of human relationships. It helps me get my sense of responsibility about my personal health into perspective. To be at peace with oneself is a desirable goal but that goal can only be achieved if one keeps the 'self' where it ought to be – in the right place and in relationship with others. Otherwise one could become an egocentric health fanatic, always fussing about whether or not one was doing the right thing to preserve or regain one's health.

Under certain circumstances it is all too easy to become preoccupied with ourselves. Living in the Western world, where, on the whole, we have too much food, too little exercise, too much stress and too little peace and quiet, it is easy to become a health fanatic. There are certainly plenty of signs that the health industry, particularly in relation to food and exercise, is highly dependent upon our collective guilt about our relative neglect of our bodies.

We can become very interested indeed in making sure that we are asking the right questions. For instance, we can get quite obsessive about whether or not there is too much salt in our food, too many additives or not enough vitamins, too much animal fat or not enough calories. We can come up with answers that persuade us to spend a lot of time, energy and money on buying or preparing special foods, whereas a little moderation in our eating habits would achieve equally good results. It is very easy, I think, to get preoccupied with ourselves. If this happens our own mental health can suffer and we are also likely to irritate those around us by our self-centred fussiness.

To be concerned about one's health is obviously good in some ways. We may, for instance, be induced to do things that are really beneficial. We may, for instance, give up eating so much animal fat, thus reducing our risk of dying of a heart attack or high blood pressure at an early age. Or we may decide to give up smoking and reduce our chances of dying from lung cancer, bronchitis or emphysema. Or we may decide to limit our alcohol intake, especially during pregnancy. However, even this has its obvious dangers in that we can become so neurotic about our health that we fail to enjoy life.

Alternatively, we can react against the health industry and the more authoritarian statements of the medical profession and neglect our health. We can eat too much, drink too much, smoke too much, and dig ourselves early graves with our abandonment to pleasure. It's a matter of keeping everything in proportion, and of deciding how we want to live our lives.

So I want to take a look at some of the more neglected ways of helping God to keep us healthy, to regain our functional health when we are ill and to move towards wholeness. I shall look at these areas separately here, although they obviously overlap in real life.

129

Keeping Healthy

God who has given us our bodies has a right to expect us to take care of them, but how often do we do that? I certainly take care of myself whenever my conscience assails me, but my conscience only works sporadically! It is, however, sharpened by the idea that I ought to try to keep as well as I can for the sake of my own children and grandchildren, and for the extended family of the community with whom I live: and for me, as a person of faith, still more so by the belief that I need to keep well for God's sake. Christopher Hamel Cooke, who founded the St Marylebone Centre for Healing, tells us that 'Health is for God', so why shouldn't you and I begin to take our health more seriously? After all, it's not much use praying to God and then doing everything we can to undermine what God is doing for us.

So, if we want to take our health seriously, where do we begin? By making a review of oneself ('begin with oneself' as Martin Buber suggests in the words I quoted at the beginning of this section). We need to do that in the spirit of Buber's prayer.

It is fairly easy to look at all the different facets of oneself – body, mind and spirit – quite systematically. If you are 'at peace with yourself' in all those areas of your being, you are probably functioning as a healthy person. However, beware. We can often feel very well in ourselves, provided we can 'keep ourselves to ourselves' and don't have to relate to other people. This is, of course, a false sense of well-being. If we can't get on with others, then ultimately we shall find ourselves unhealthy. So we have to extend our review to our relationships, both with other people and with God, or whatever we hold on to as our ideal. If you're still 'at peace', count yourself very fortunate and thank God for it. If not, then you, like me, will need to do what you can to move towards becoming a more whole person. That is someone who has integrated the various aspects of your being – including all the physical, mental and emotional 'opposites' in you – into a harmonious unity, so that you can function well as a person and relate well to those among whom you live and work.

In planning how you're going to do this, you will probably want to look at all kinds of books and take advice about what you can do to preserve and improve your health. Enough has been written about the role of diet, exercise and relaxation in keeping healthy. You should be able to find what you need quite easily, so I'm not going to focus on those areas here. Instead, I want to go back to a more neglected aspect of human life, certainly as it is lived in our Western world. I want to go back to the idea of Avalon, about which Tennyson wrote in the poem I quoted at the beginning of this chapter. His poem points me to something I cannot get from books, nor even from relaxation and relief of stress. He points me to the need to feed my soul.

Even when I'm functionally healthy, and particularly perhaps when I'm feeling 'on top of the world', I need beauty, stillness and silence to 'heal me of my grievous wound', whatever that may be. (There is always a 'wound' even though it may be simply the wound of being a human being.) I need to find places and people who are at peace within themselves. Just being at places like the poet's Avalon, or being with people who are whole, enables me to get in touch with an inner stillness which is healing.

Each of us will have our own Avalon: a secluded garden, a special tree, a comfortable armchair, a peaceful room in a friend's house, a dark corner in a church, maybe even a convent chapel. Wherever it is, it is somewhere we can go to, not only in our body, but also in the reality of our waking dreams. There in our own special place or places – for there may very well be more than one Avalon – we find that renewal and recreation just happen, without any strain.

There are people, too, who give me that sense of peace. Just to be with them is good. So when I find myself restless or unhappy or 'out of sorts', all of which I count as normal for someone who is healthy, I will try to be near them. I once had a doctor who could make me feel better almost at once. I and some of his other patients used to laugh about it from time to time. He achieved this just by being himself, and by the way he wanted us to get better and to keep healthy. We did our very best to fulfil his expectations, simply in order that he should not be disappointed. Almost as soon as you walked into his presence you

131

felt better. If I can't get to such a person or a trusted friend, I will often write to a friend who gives me that feeling of being at home in himself or herself. Doing that will bring me into contact with a peace outside myself and by the end of the letter I often feel much better.

Searching for Avalon is one of the most important things we can do to help God to keep us healthy. It involves taking adequate rest and making sure we get holidays, even if the only thing we can afford to do is walk in a park. Avalon will be there waiting for us if we have the desire to find it. To search for Avalon is like going on a pilgrimage. There has to be an air of excitement as one sets out on the journey. Yet the end is so often found in the journey itself. In that sense Avalon is like the Ithaca of which the poet Cavafy wrote:

> When you set out on your journey to Ithaca
> Then pray that the road is long, full of adventure, full of
>   knowledge . . .
> Always keep Ithaca fixed in your mind.
> To arrive there is your ultimate goal.
> But do not hurry the voyage at all.
> It is better to let it last for long years;
> And even to anchor at the isle when you are old,
> Rich with all that you have gained on the way,
> Not expecting that Ithaca will offer you riches.[5]

Our Avalons, our Ithacas, beckon us, whether they be places, or people, or God. It is our search that keeps us healthy, even though it may sometimes seem to be interrupted by illness.

Recovering Functional Health

When we are ill most of us lose sight of Avalon, or Ithaca. The illness itself envelops us like the tentacles of an octopus. Nor is it at all easy to enter the stage of convalescence. People tell us we are getting better, but we don't feel that we are. Or they tell us we are not getting better and confirm our worst fears. It is possible to lose the desire to recover. Being ill becomes more attractive than struggling to get well, for being well will bring back all the stress we had to contend with before.

It is when we are ill that we most need other people, and, paradoxically, it is then that we so often find ourselves driving them away. Jennifer Rees Larcombe speaks movingly about this in her book, *Beyond Healing*. She drove people away until she became quite isolated. Mercifully she had the humility to realise what she was doing and she stopped and fought her way back into relationships with all kinds of people.

There is no easy way back to functional health. Whenever we are injured or ill we do become dependent on other people. In a sense this is inevitable and right. Suppose, for instance, that you are driving your car on the motorway. Suddenly another car swerves across the crash barrier and hits the side of your car at speed. The moment before the accident you were in full control of your destiny. Now, you are not. You find yourself trapped and injured but still conscious.

Suddenly you are helpless. You are dependent for your very survival on other people. Firemen will come and cut you free from the wreckage. Ambulance men will arrive to take you to hospital. The police will redirect the traffic and you may even have to watch helplessly while they take statements from witnesses. When you eventually arrive at the hospital a team of doctors and nurses will take over and for a time you will become wholly dependent on them for medical care, food and drink, even washing and toileting. At this stage you need to remain dependent in order to allow other people to do for you what you cannot possibly do for yourself. Moveover this dependency will also extend to your relatives. They too will find themselves relatively passive during the early stages. So long as your recovery is taking place, you and they will probably remain relatively dependent, until you begin to convalesce.

If your progress seems to be slow, or something goes really wrong, then you may still be helpless, but your relatives may have to begin asking awkward questions. They may have to share in making decisions which will affect you and may even determine whether you live or die. That balance between a proper dependency and a proper retention of autonomy is difficult to achieve. Getting it right can make all the difference to your recovery. Getting it wrong can delay your healing, or even work against it.

I have used an extreme example to illustrate the reality of dependency in injury or illness, but this problem of how to balance dependency and autonomy is one which occurs – to a greater or lesser degree – in all illnesses which are serious enough to leave one unable to work for more than a few days. I want to leave the kind of dependency that comes upon us all as we age and/or come to die until later. Meanwhile, suppose that you are recovering well from your accidental injuries and have reached the stage of convalescence.

As you get better you will begin to want to take control of your life again. This happens at different rates for different individuals. The move from full dependency to full independence is fraught with difficulties. In the initial stages, when you still need quite a bit of help, you will need the humility to accept that help without clinging on to it, to use it as a stepping stone and not as a crutch. Convalescence can be a horrible time. Although other people tend to tell you that you are better, you may very well feel worse. Your feelings simply don't match their expectations. The struggle back to functional health seems quite impossible.

I have fought this battle myself, not once but several times, after long and debilitating illnesses. The road to recovery seemed very long and hard, and I don't expect I was at all patient with myself over it, but the experience of prolonged incapacity has been valuable. I have found two strategies that have been really helpful. I do not think I would have found them without the help of understanding relatives and close friends, good professional advisers and the services of the Church.

The first of these is that when I am really ill, and feel that I am about to be devoured by the illness, I surrender my autonomy and accept every scrap of help that is offered to me with deep thankfulness. I even go so far as to realise that I can't pray when I am in such a condition of helplessness. I need to be rescued by

God and I need God to send someone to me to untangle me if possible. I may still be able to utter a few childhood prayers, but sometimes I can't even remember the Lord's Prayer. Then I know that I need to rely on other people's prayers. I also need the reassurance that I am worth praying for and with. In that way I am very like Michael Mayne (whom I quoted in the last chapter), in wanting to be touched and also given the spoken assurance of God's love for me. When I am ill I am quite bold about this. To save priests and other Christian friends the embarrassment of trying to decide whether or not their ministry is acceptable to me, I ask for it straight out. If I didn't want this kind of help I should say so. Then my visitors would know what to do. I wish that more people could bring themselves to this degree of honesty, but when we are ill we sometimes find it difficult to mobilise even this amount of energy.

It is when I am on the verge of getting better that I find it hardest to know what I really want. It is then that I use the second strategy. I am one of those people who need to express my inward feelings by outward action. So I go to a healing service and I wait for the Holy Spirit to tell me whether or not I am prepared to get out of my seat, walk to the front of the church and receive the laying on of hands. At any healing service God always retains the initiative. God can heal us, just like that. At any time I may find myself completely restored to health and 'ready to go'. I know that. But more often than not God wants my co-operation, my willingness to take up the responsibility of being well, and so this simple action of moving tells me whether or not I am ready for that move towards the interdependence of being well again. There have been times when I have known that I am not ready and then I have stayed in my seat. There have been other times when I have not wanted to be healed, but have known that God thinks I ought to be ready. Then I have reluctantly got to my feet and walked down the aisle. And there have been times when I have been full of rejoicing and almost leapt to my feet simply to celebrate recovery.

These two strategies work for me. They may not do so for you, but it is worth looking for something similar of your own devising. I have simply offered them as a model of how we can co-operate with God's work in very simple practical ways.

There are lots of others. For instance, I remember that during a period of depression after a bereavement I set myself a goal of going on pilgrimage by a certain date. I took the precaution of asking a friend to go with me because that would make it harder for me to opt out. Then I fought the black moods by projecting myself firmly into the future. I had chosen something I wanted to do very much and had invested a considerable sum of money in advance, so that strong incentive helped me to get through a particularly grim period. That might not work for someone else. Each person needs to work out their own strategies in the light of their personal circumstances.

In the end there does come a day when one is suddenly conscious that the battle is won. The joy of being alive has returned, transiently at first, then more frequently and surely. Health has returned even though the healing has to go on until we become whole. And that, as we know, is a lifetime's task.

Moving Towards Wholeness

If you want to become a whole person in the forward-looking sense – that is a person who fulfils your potential – you will need to have some clear idea about who you have been, who you are, and who you are becoming.

When we are growing up, most of us want to emulate a role model: perhaps a football star, a beauty queen, a life-saving doctor or a powerful politician. As we grow into maturity we accept the fact that very few people ever achieve that sort of fame or success. We become less sure that our role models' lives are really so desirable. We begin to enjoy who we are. We recognise our limitations. We begin to find it possible to incorporate defect, physical, mental and emotional liabilities and uglinesses of various sorts, into ourselves. We begin to be content to be who we are, rather than who we were, or who we thought we were. Yet we remain conscious that we are becoming; that is that we are still growing towards the completion of our lives, a completion that will be found in and through and after death.

My own role model ever since I was eighteen years old has been God-made-man in the person of Christ. But my idea of what it means to become more like that person has changed as I have moved from hero worship to the acceptance of God's action in helping me grow towards wholeness. In the end I hope to become the person that God wants me to become, a person who is 'like' Christ, yet uniquely the person whom God made me to be.

In the task of becoming fully human, the person God wants us to be, I feel that the initiative must lie with God, whether or not you and I recognise that mysterious presence at work in us. As far as I'm concerned I shall grow towards becoming fully human by listening to what God is doing in creation, listening to God in the stillness of prayer, listening to God through the pages of the Bible, listening to other people's wisdom, listening to the whispering that goes on in the depths of myself. That is my own tradition, but I feel strongly that people of all faiths, and none, can draw on their own resources in the same kind of way. Everyone has an ideal which he or she needs to pursue in order to be fully alive and healthy. My ideal is enshrined in the word God, even though the closer I get to God the less I am able to describe what I mean by that word.

Since God is always leading and we are always following, we can feel safe in God's hands, but I also find it very helpful to have a soul friend with whom I can share what is happening to me. In that way I can protect myself from chasing 'mirages' or false gods, and concentrate instead on following in Christ's foot- steps, being content to go slowly or fast, at God's pace rather than mine.

Soul friends are rather special people. A soul friend is someone with whom one can share all the best and all the worst of oneself without shame. He or she is someone whom we see regularly, who loves us enough to want us to grow and who challenges us if we aren't going in the right direction. A soul friend should be someone sufficiently widely read to be able to point us to the food we need for our spiritual growth. We need to be able to trust them, but not to be so dependent on them that we follow them slavishly. Soul friends need to be sufficiently tuned in to our particular wavelength to be sympathetic to our way of thinking and praying. But they should also be sufficiently different from us to allow us to follow our own path and not theirs. A soul friend is not an old-style spiritual director, nor is he or she a psychotherapist, or any other kind of therapist. You may need help from someone else as well, but you should be clear about the difference. Soul friends do not need to be priests, or ministers of religion, or even Christians, though Christians usually prefer to go to people of their own faith. Having said that, two of my close friends regularly visit a learned and holy Hindu who understands their own kind of journey better than anyone else has ever done.

Finding a soul friend is quite a responsibility. Sometimes one has to wait a long time before the right person turns up, but it is remarkable how they do if you want to find someone and keep your eyes and ears open. You may not need a soul friend at all. You may need more than one. On this journey to wholeness you may have a network of friends who are either healers themselves or in tune with your needs. Or you may find that you can pick up what you need from books and radio or television programmes. The point I am making is that it is good to have someone around who can act as a point of reference from time to time. But the journey is yours and no one else's, and you are the person who has to take charge of that journey. At least that is true for a large part of your life, but not when you draw towards its end.

When we become sick, or as we grow older, it is far less easy to remain in charge. One of the most difficult stages in life comes when we begin to notice signs of our own mortality and realise that we must die. Most of us, I think, do not fear death so much as the whole process of dying, which includes loss of autonomy, diminishments in our strength and abilities, and the humiliation of having to be cared for in our simplest bodily needs. Pierre Teilhard de Chardin helps me greatly with his insight into this phase of living. He writes:

138

When the signs of age begin to mark my body (and still more when they touch my mind); when the ill that is to diminish me or carry me off strikes from without or is born within me; when the painful moment comes in which I suddenly awaken to the fact that I am ill or growing old; and above all at that last moment when I feel I am losing hold of myself and am absolutely passive within the hands of the great unknown forces that have formed me; in all these dark moments, O God, grant that I may understand that it is you (provided only my faith is strong enough) who are painfully parting the fibres of my being in order to penetrate to the very marrow of my substance and bear me away within yourself.[6]

How can we move towards wholeness when we are dying? An Anglican priest, W. H. Vanstone, has written movingly about the passivities of old age and life-threatening illnesses. He points out that:

It is not necessarily the case that a man is most fully human when he is achiever rather than receiver, active rather than passive, subject rather than object of what is happening.[7]

In this and other passages in his book, *The Stature of Waiting*, Vanstone is saying that all human beings are persons of dignity, that passivity cannot prevent us from growth and that the prospect of death is an invitation to continue to grow. The poet, John Donne, invites us to reflect on death before we go through that door:

Since I am coming to that holy room,
Where, with thy quire of saints for evermore,
I shall be made thy Music; as I come
I tune the instrument here at the door,
And what I must do then, think here before.[8]

Perhaps one of the best preparations we can make for dying is to reflect on our lives, perhaps even to write something down about them for our children and close friends. If we do that I think we shall find much to celebrate and much to share, even if we also have some painful memories to recall and quite a lot of forgiving to do as well. That kind of work helps us to get ready for the actual dying we all have to do, a dying which is also a healing.

I have watched many people die. Some have been close relatives, others friends, others patients. Very often it has felt as if we were all waiting for a birth. As a mother I was always aware that once I was pregnant there was no way back to what I had been before that moment of fertilisation. Whether the pregnancy went to term or ended prematurely there would be a birth. My own wishes in the matter were no longer relevant. Even if I wanted to I could do nothing to stop it. It would happen. The outcome would be an occasion for joy or sorrow. Pregnancy would end in labour and labour in birth. So the best way to manage myself during those long months of waiting during pregnancy, and the short but intense work of labour, was to surrender to the creative forces that had taken me over and were stronger than I. I think that I shall have to do the same when my time comes to die: surrender, and allow myself to flow into it. And as I do that and let go of the shore of life to swim out into the deep waters of God's love I hope that I shall be able to look back and know how much I love the people I leave behind and how much they love me. That degree of sharing seems to be of God. It is something the Father seems to have allowed to His Son, who died with his mother and his close friend nearby. It is something I too hope for when I die. But I am not yet so close to that point. There may yet be a lot of living to do, and while I am alive I am also in relationship with other people. My healing, my movement towards wholeness, must take account of the relationship John Donne speaks about when he says 'no man is an Island, entire of it self'.

Martin Buber's prayer, which I used at the very beginning of this section, points the way forward. He asks us to 'begin with oneself, but not to end with oneself'. I have found that any serious reflection on my own state of health invariably leads me to reflect on my relationships with other people and with society in general. I don't count myself well unless I am also at peace with God, and I can't be at peace with God unless I am sharing the healing God shares with me. That means accepting a further responsibility.

Taking Responsibility for Others

It is a truism to say that we live in a global village, yet no less important for that. We are made to be whole. We are also made to help others become whole. That is a task which can be fulfilled in a number of ways. I have spent a lot of my life trying to contribute not only to the health of individuals, but also to the health of the society in which I live, and today that means not only my own community or country, but also those in other parts of the world.

Like most people, the ways in which I do these things are small. I try to support political initiatives that take disadvantaged people in my own country, and those in the poor countries of the world seriously. I try to use environment-friendly washing powders. I try not to pollute the atmosphere with ozone-destroying sprays. I try not to use pesticides in the garden that will destroy wildlife. I try to use recycled writing paper. I try to buy goods from small co-operatives in the remote and poorer areas of our world. I take clothes to our local Oxfam or Save the Children shops, and I try to support them in other ways.

All these are very small things to do, but if a lot of us do them, they contribute, I believe, to the health of the world and the universe. And in more specific ways I continue to rejoice in the ways in which other people and I can contribute to the healing of individuals through the healing ministry.

I have already spoken about the way in which the Japanese doctor, Dr Nagai, shared his wholeness with me through the pages of a book. I have also written about the way in which very handicapped children and people have helped to heal me. When we are healed we are so grateful to God that we often want to share what we have been given. And it does seem as if the more we have been given, the more we have to share. Dorothy Kerin, for example, devoted the whole of her life to the Christian healing ministry after she had been miraculously healed. Martin Israel's personal ministry began after he had been suddenly and quite unexpectedly healed from an

141

unpleasant sinus complaint. God seems to give each person a particular charism, a particular work, which only he or she can do. And the work is as varied as the people. In every case, however, the work is done on behalf of other people.

Many people who are involved in healing ministries are not Christians. All, I believe, are doing God's work, with the exception of the charlatans who ride on the backs of the authentic carers. I respect the work of all disinterested persons who are engaged in healing work, but I write about the Christian healing ministry because I know it at first hand.

What constantly amazes me is the dedication of the people whom God involves in this work. I think of Dame Cicely Saunders, for instance, who started her working life as a hospital almoner, became a nurse and then found herself studying medicine. When she qualified she devoted herself to the care of dying patients, raised hundreds of thousands of pounds to build St Christopher's Hospice, and extended her teaching about pain control and the care of dying patients far beyond its walls. In a long career she has taught thousands of doctors and nurses, shared the vision which God gave her with countless people and brought healing to the whole of society.[9]

I think also of William Kyle, a Methodist minister, and Bonita, his wife, who founded the Westminster Pastoral Foundation at the Central Methodist Hall in Westminster (see p. 155). Against heavy opposition at the time from people who felt that clergymen shouldn't be involved in professional counselling, William Kyle developed a highly respected service which is available to anyone who needs it. By the time of his early death its influence had extended all over Britain. The Westminster counsellors are highly trained to professional standards and there is excellent co-operation between them and psychiatrists.

God gives strength to women, like Dame Cicily, and to men, like William Kyle; the strength to carry out their vision and the colleagues they need to expand their work. We all owe such people a great debt. They do not work only for Christians, but for the whole of society and we all benefit from their vision. They are exceptional people. We can't all be like them, but we can draw strength from their example and our own healing, and share our own insights with those with whom we are in contact. Yes, our ways are small. We visit someone in hospital. We look after someone's baby. We take a few flowers to a lonely person. We listen, and listen, and listen. We may discover that we need some training so that we can listen more intently and more wisely. There are many and various courses open to anyone who wants to learn more about healing and about specific healing ministries. They can be found both in the Christian healing ministry and in organisations like the Samaritans and Relate. These are the kinds of ways in which we can take part in God's work. And in all these different but interlinked ways we shall find that we are being invited to receive what God offers us so that we can share God's gifts of healing with other people. When we have done it for a while we shall find that we are becoming who we are meant to be. And we shall thank God and rejoice.

Healing is infectious. A small stone dropped into a pool of water makes ripples. The breath of God spreads them right to the very edge of the pool. In the end all healing comes from God, and all those who are being made whole go to God. We are enclosed in God's wholeness and thus made whole ourselves. So I end with a prayer of St Anselm, who lived in the eleventh century. He sums up what I feel to be my prayer to God at the end of the twentieth century:

I pray, O God that I know you and love you, so that I may rejoice in you. And if I cannot do so fully in this life, may I progress every day until all comes to fullness; let the knowledge of you grow in me here in this life, and there in heaven let it be complete; let your love grow in me here and reach fullness there, so that here my joy may be great in hope and there be complete in reality.

Until then, let my mind meditate on you, let my tongue speak of you, let my heart love you, let my mouth preach you. Let my soul hunger for you, let my flesh thirst for you, my whole being desire you, until I enter the joy of the Lord, who is God, Three in One, blessed for ever.[10]

Notes and Further Reading

All Biblical references are taken from the New Revised Standard Version.

INTRODUCTION
1   Izaak Walton, *Compleat Angler*, 1653, Chapter 21.

CHAPTER 1 UNCOVERING SOME TRUTHS ABOUT HEALING
1   David Jenkins in lecture, quoted in James McGilvray's *The Quest for Health and Wholeness*, The German Institute for Medical Missions, 1981, p.xiii.
2   Ibid, p.xii.
3   See Chapter 6, p.98.
4   See Chapter 6, p.98 for Ayurvedic healing and Chapter 3 for transcendental meditation (TM).
5   Technical term for orthodox Western-style medicine which uses drugs to alleviate symptoms of disease. To be distinguished from homeopathic medicine. See Chapter 6, p.99.
6   An example is TM, an ancient Indian technique for meditation, which was introduced into America in 1961 by the Maharishi mahesh Yogi, from where it spread worldwide.
7   For brief notes on all these therapies, see Chapter 6, pp.98–102.
8   James 5:13–18.
9   Evelyn Frost, *Christian Healing*, A. R. Mowbray Ltd, 1940; and Morton Kelsey, *Healing and Christianity*, SCM Press Ltd, 1973.
10   Evelyn Frost, op. cit., pp.175–195; and see Stephen Pattinson, *Alive and Kicking*, SCM Press Ltd, 1989, pp.46–54 for a concise overview of the history of Christian healing.
11   Franz Werfel *The Song of Bernadette*, Hamish Hamilton, 1942.
12   St Thérèse of Lisieux, *Story of a Soul*, trans. by Ronald Knox, Harvill Press, 1958.
13   Dorothy Arnold, *Dorothy Kerin*, Burrswood Publications, 1965, p.11.

14   See Chapter 8, p.217 and Christopher Hamel Cooke, *Health is for God*, Arthur James, 1986, pp.93–98.

15   Walter J. Hollenweger, *The Pentecostals*, SCM Press Ltd, 1972.

16   See 1 Corinthians 12, and also Chapters 13 and 14 which put the charismatic gifts into the context of the 'more excellent way' of love.

17   See Francis MacNutt, *Healing*, Ave Maria Press, 1974, pp.9–15; Agnes Sandford, *Healing Gifts of the Spirit*, Arthur James, 1966; and Kathryn Kuhlman, *I Believe in Miracles*, Oliphants, 1962.

18   George Bennett, *Miracle at Crowhurst*, Arthur James, 1970; *The Heart of Healing*, Arthur James, 1971; *In His Healing Steps*, Arthur James, 1976.

19   Francis MacNutt, *Healing*, Ave Maria Press, 1974; *The Power to Heal*, Ave Maria Press, 1975.

20   David Watson, *Fear No Evil*, Hodder & Stoughton, 1984.

21   John Wimber, *Power Healing*, Hodder & Stoughton, 1986.

22   Colin Urquhart, *Receive Your Healing*, Hodder & Stoughton, 1986.

23   R. D. Hacking, *Such a Strange Journey*, A. R. Mowbray Ltd, 1988.

24   John Richards, *But Deliver Us From Evil*, Darton, Longman & Todd, 1974.

25   *The Churches Ministry of Healing*, Church Information Board, 1958.

26   Morris Maddocks, *The Christian Healing Ministry*, Society for Promoting Christian Knowledge, 1981.

27   Ibid., pp.167–169.

28   R. S. Lambourne, *Community, Church and Healing*, Darton, Longman & Todd, 1973.

29   Michael Wilson, *The Church is Healing*, SCM, 1966; and *Health is for People*, Darton, Longman & Todd, 1975.

30   James McGilvray, op. cit.

31   Michael Wilson, *Health is for People*, pp.17ff and pp.79ff.

Chapter 2 Wholeness, Disease and Healing

1   An Indian author, poet and philosopher who won the Nobel prize for literature in 1913 for his book of poems, *Gitanjali*. This quote is from *Stray Birds*, Macmillan & Co., 1941, p.42.

2   John Keats, *Endymion*, Book 1, 1, 1ff.

3   Alfred, Lord Tennyson, *Poems*, Christopher Ricks (ed.) Longmans Green, 1969, p.1193, No. 349.

4   Ecclesiastes 3:1.

5   Ibid., 3:10–11.

6   Teilhard de Chardin, *The Phenomenon of Man*, Collins, 1982, p.291.

7   G. Carter and T. Karris, *From Protest to Challenge*, Vol. 2, Hoover Institute Press, 1977, p.301.

8   W. H. Auden and L. Kronenberger (eds.), *Faber Book of Aphorisms*, 1964, p.217.

9   Romans 8:19–21.

10   Ephesians 6:11–12.

11   Matthew Fox, *Original Blessing*, Bear & Co. Inc., Santa Fe, New Mexico, 1983.

12   Rahe and Arthur, *A Longitudinal Study of Life Change and Illness Patterns, Journal of Psychosomatic Research*, 1967, Vol. 10, pp.355–66.

13   Alvin Toffler, *Future Shock*, Bodley Head, 1972, p.295.

14   See HRH Prince Charles' preface to Patrick Pietroni, *The Greening of Medicine*. Victor Gollancz Ltd, 1990; and also p.181–2 in the same book.

15   See, for instance, Mary Craig, *Blessings*, Hodder and Stoughton, 1979; Frances Young, *Face to Faith*, James Clarke, 1980; and Margaret Spufford, *Celebration*, Collins Fount, 1989.

16   Quoted in T. C. Simcox, *A Treasury of Quotations on Christian Themes*, Society for Promoting Christian Knowledge, 1976.

17   Michael Buckley, *His Healing Touch*, Collins Fount, 1987, p.13.

18   A noted writer, translator, retreat conductor and exponent of the mystical life, who wrote a classic study, *Mysticism*, Methuen & Co., 1911. In her later years she was a pacifist.

19   T. C. Simcox, op. cit., No. 2106.

20   Paul Glynn, *A Song for Nagasaski*, Catholic Book Club, Australia, 1988, and Collins Fount, 1990.

21   Ibid., p.176.

22   Ibid., p.189.

23   Ibid., p.190.

24   Ibid., p.219.

CHAPTER 3 IN TUNE WITH NATURE

1   *Oxford Dictionary of Quotations*, Oxford University Press, 2nd Edition, 1953, p.191.

2   Ernest Rutherford (1871–1953) was a New Zealand-born British

scientist, whose researches into the structure of the atomic nucleus won him the Nobel prize for chemistry in 1928.

3   Albert Einstein (1879–1955), the German-born US physicist whose relativity theory revolutionised concepts of space and time, was awarded the Nobel prize for physics in 1921.

4   Niels Bohr (1855–1962) was a Danish physicist who used quantum theory to explain Rutherford's research findings. He stated that the leap from one orbit to another is accompanied by the emission or absorption of a quantum (a measured amount) of energy. He was awarded the Nobel prize for physics in 1921.

5   Fritjof Capra is an Austrian-born physicist who researches theoretical high energy physics in the USA. He has written about the relationship between modern physics and Eastern mysticism in *The Tao of Physics*, Wildwood House, 1975, and Fontana, 1976.

6   Fritjof Capra, *The Tao of Physics*, p.59ff.

7   Ibid., p.148ff.

8   Ibid., p.236ff.

9   Ibid., p.69ff.

10   Ibid., p.71.

11   Ibid., p.83.

12   Quatum: a discrete amount of some quantity, especially of energy or angular momentum by which a system might change.

13   John Polkinghorne, formerly Cambridge Professor of Mathematical Physics, is now President of Queen's College, Cambridge. For his differences from Capra, see *Science and Creation*, Society for Promoting Christian Knowledge, 1988.

14   See Chapter 3, p.80 and Una Kroll, *TM a Signpost for the World*, Darton, Longman & Todd, 1974, p.71–94.

15   Deepak Chopra, *Quantum Healing*, Bantam Books, 1989.

16   Fritjof Capra, *The Tao of Physics*, p.144–166.

17   Ibid., pp.83ff.

18   Deepak Chopra, *Quantum Healing*, p.46ff.

19   John Polkinghorne, *Science and Creation*, p.44–45.

20   Fritjof Capra, *The Tao of Physics*, p.236.

21   Ibid., p.258.

22   John Polkinghorne, *Science and Creation*, p.74.

23   Lyall Watson, *Beyond Supernature*, Hodder & Stoughton, 1986, p.108.

24   Ibid., p.238.

25   Chris Belshaw, *Osteopathy. Is it for you?* Element Books Ltd, 1987, p.22.

26   Susan Moore, *New Ways to Health. A Guide to Chiropractic*. Hamlyn Publishing Group, 1988, p.126.
27   Alexander MacDonald, *Acupuncture*, George Allen & Unwin, 1982, p.166.
28   Girard W. Cambell, DO, *A Doctor's Proven New Home Cure for Arthritis*, Thorsons Publishers Ltd, 1979.
29   Nicola Hall, *Reflexology, a Way to Better Health*, Pan Books, 1988 and Chapter 6, p.155.
30   Interview with BBC, 1991.
31   Anne Alcock o.p., *Reflections*, Ennismore Publications, 1989, St Dominic's Priory, Montenotte, Cork, Ireland.
32   James 5:14–16.
33   Work of S. Krippner and D. Rubin in 1973, quoted in Norman Autton, *Touch – an exploration*. Darton, Longman & Todd, 1989, pp.132–133.
34   Work of D. Keiger quoted in ibid., pp.134–136.
35   Ibid., 1989.

CHAPTER 4 PSYCHIC SENSITIVITY
1   Sir Arthur Eddington, a British astronomer and physicist, was an early exponent of the theory of relativity. Quoted in Lyall Watson, *Supernature*, Hodder & Stoughton, 1973, p.239.
2   Ibid., p.249.
3   See Norman Autton, op. cit., p.135; and Deepak Chopra, op. cit., pp.165–169.
4   T. S. Eliot, *Four Quartets*, Complete Edition, Faber & Faber, 1969, p.192.
5   Lyall Watson, *Beyond Supernature*, p.157.
6   Martin Israel, *The Quest for Wholeness*, Darton, Longman & Todd, 1989, pp.75–76.

CHAPTER 5 TOUCHING THE SPIRITUAL
1   Gilbert Shaw, *The Face of Love*, A. R. Mowbray, 1959, p.221. Adapted for card by SLG Press, Fairacres Convent, date unknown.
2   Jumbulance: a jumbo-sized ambulance.
3   See Morton Kelsey, *Healing and Christianity*, SCM Press, 1973. The New Testament records 41 healings by Jesus.
4   Brother Lawrence, *The Practice of the Presence of God*, A. R. Mowbray Ltd, 1977, p.47.
5   Gilbert Shaw, op. cit., p.221.

6   Matthew 6:6.

7   Joni Eareckson, *Joni*, Pickering & Inglis, 1978; and *A Step Further*, Pickering & Inglis, 1979.

8   Jennifer Rees Larcombe, *Beyond Healing*, Hodder & Stoughton, 1986, p.111.

9   Matthew 18:20.

10   Article in *Renewal*, October 1990, Broadway House, The Broadway, Crowborough, East Sussex.

11   Ibid.

12   Interview with BBC, 1991.

13   David Watson, op. cit., p.172.

14   Matthew 8:5–13.

15   1 Corinthians 12:4–11.

16   *Book of Common Prayer*, 1662, p.356.

17   Matthew 6:13.

18   1 Peter 5:8.

CHAPTER 6 GETTING IN TOUCH WITH OUR NEED

1   Grace Sheppard, *An Aspect of Fear*, Darton, Longman & Todd, 1989, p.7.

2   Ibid., p.1.

3   Ibid., p.xi.

4   Ibid., p.8.

5   T. C. Simcox, op. cit., No. 1074.

6   Anne Townsend in an interview with the BBC, 1991.

7   Ibid.

8   Ibid.

9   John Chapin (ed.), *Book of Catholic Quotations*, John Calder, 1957, p.428.

10   Patrick Pietroni, *The Greening of Medicine*, Victor Gollancz Ltd, 1990, pp.171–186.

11   Philippians 4:11b–14.

12   Jennifer Rees Larcombe, Interview with the BBC, 1991.

13   Michael Mayne, *A Year Lost and Found*, Darton, Longman & Todd, 1987.

14   Ibid., p.15.

CHAPTER 7 WHEN THINGS GO WRONG

1   Leo Rosten, *Treasury of Jewish Quotations* W.H. Allen, 1973, p.485.

2 Elizabeth D. Ward, *Timbo*, Sidgwick & Jackson, 1986.
3 Christy Nolan, *Dam-burst of Dreams*, Weidenfeld & Nicolson Ltd. 1981; and *Under the Eye of the Clock*, Weidenfeld & Nicolson, 1988.
4 Mary Craig, op. cit.
5 Frances Young, op. cit.
6 Margaret Spufford, op. cit.
7 Jane Grayshon, *A Pathway through Pain*, Kingsway Publications, 1987.
8 Ibid., p.47.
9 Ibid., p.156.
10 James Woodward (ed.) *Embracing the Chaos*, SPCK, 1990, p.116.
11 Ibid., p.117.
12 BBC interview, 1991.
13 BBC interview, 1991.
14 Raymond Studzinski, *Concilium*, April 1986, Stichting Concilium and T & T Clark Ltd, pp.12–21.
15 Ibid., p.15.
16 Ibid., p.17.
17 Stanley Hauerwas, *Suffering Presence*, University of Notre Dame Press, 1986, p.186.
18 Romans 8:24–25.

CHAPTER 8 TAKING RESPONSIBILITY
1 Alfred, Lord Tennyson, *The Idylls of the King*, Frederick Warne & Co, 1909, pp.473–4.
2 Christopher Hamel Cooke, op. cit., p.7.
3 Andrew Norman, *Silence in God*, Society for Promoting Christian Knowledge, 1970, p.137.
4 Martin Buber, *Form of Prayer for Jewish Worship*, Vol. 1. 1977.
5 P. J. Cavafy, *Collected Poems*, trans. by Rae Dalvern, Harcourt, Brace, Jovanovich Inc., 1948, p.36.
6 Teilhard de Chardin, *Le Milieu Divin*, Collins, 1960, p.69.
7 W. H. Vanstone, *The Stature of Waiting*, Darton, Longman & Todd, 1982, p.50.
8 John Donne, 'Hymne to God in my Sickness', in R. S. Thomas (ed.), *Penguin Book of Verse*, 1963, p.33.
9 Shirley de Bouley, *Cicely Saunders*, Hodder & Stoughton, 1984.
10 St Anselm, *Prayers and Meditations*, trans. by Benedicta Ward, Penguin Books, 1973, p.266.

Some Useful Books

In addition to the books mentioned in the Notes I have found the following helpful:

General

ALASTAIR CAMPBELL, *A Dictionary of Pastoral Care*, Society for Promoting Christian Knowledge, 1987.

EDGAR JACKSON, *The Role of Faith in the Process of Healing*, SCM Ltd, 1981.

FRANCIS MACNUTT, *The Power to Heal*, Ave Maria Press, 1977.

MORRIS MADDOCKS, *A Healing House of Prayer* Hodder & Stoughton, 1987.

MORRIS MADDOCKS, *Twenty Questions about Healing*, Society for Promoting Christian Knowledge, 1988.

Pastoral

NORMAN AUTTON, *Pain*, Darton, Longman & Todd, 1986.

HOWARD BOOTH, *Healing Experiences*, Bible Reading Fellowship, 1985.

JOYCE HUGGETT, *Listening to Others*, Hodder & Stoughton, 1988.

MARTIN ISRAEL, *Healing as Sacrament*, Darton, Longman & Todd, 1984.

MARTIN ISRAEL, *The Dark Face of Reality*, Collins Fount, 1989.

SALLY KNIGHT AND ROBERT GANN, *The Self-help Guide*, Chapman & Hall, 1988.

DENNIS AND MATTHEW LINN, *Healing of Memories*, Paulist Press, 1984.

KENNETH MCALL, *Healing the Family Tree*, Sheldon Press, 1982.

WANDA NASH, *At Ease with Stress*, Darton, Longman & Todd, 1988.

COLIN MURRAY PARKES, *Bereavement*, Penguin, 1987.

CICELY SAUNDERS, *Beyond the Horizon*, Darton, Longman & Todd, 1990.

SIMON STEPHENS, *Death Comes Home*, A. R. Mowbray, 1972.

Helpful Addresses

Alternative Medicine

Ayurvedic Medicine and Transcendental Meditation,
Freepost, London SW1P 4YY   *Tel:* 0800 269 303.

Bristol Cancer Centre,
Grove House, Cornwallis Grove,
Clifton, Bristol BS9 1SY   *Tel:* 0272 743216

British Chiropractic Association,
10, Greycoat Place, London SW1P 1SB   *Tel:* 071 222 8866.

Council and Register of Osteopaths,
56, London Street, Reading RG1 4SQ   *Tel:* 0734 576585.

Council for Acupuncture,
38, Mount Pleasant, London WC1 0AP   *Tel:* 071 837 8026.

Council for Complementary and Alternative Medicine,
38, Mount Pleasant, London WC1 0AP   *Tel:* 071 409 1440.

Diets,
British Society for Nutritional Medicine,
5, Somerhill Road, Hove, East Sussex BN3 1RP   *Tel:* 0273 722003.

Faculty of Homeopathy,
Royal London Homeopathic Hospital,
Great Ormond Street, London WC1N 3HR   *Tel:* 071 837 3091.

National Institute of Medical Herbalists,
c/o 9, Palace Gate, Exeter EX1 1JA   *Tel:* 0392 426022.

Reflexology,
Monks Orchard, Whitbourne, Worcs WR6 5RB.

Christian Healing Centres

Acorn Christian Healing Trust,
Whitehill Chase, High Street, Bordon,
Hants GU35 0AP   *Tel:* 0420 478121/472779.

Churches Council for Health and Healing,
St Marylebone Parish Church,
Marylebone Road, London NW1 5LT   *Tel:* 071 486 9644.

Divine Healing Mission,
The Old Rectory,
Crowhurst, Battle, East Sussex TN33 9AD   *Tel:* 042 483 204.

Dorothy Kevin Trust,
Burrswood, Groombridge,
Tunbridge Wells, Kent TN3 9PY   *Tel:* 0892 863637.

Green Pastures,
17 Burton Road, Branksome Park,
Bournemouth, BH13 6DT   *Tel:* 0202 764776.

Harnhill Centre of Christian Healing,
Harnhill Manor, Cirencester, Gloucs GL7 5PX   *Tel:* 0285 850283.

Counselling
British Association for Counselling,
327a Sheep Street, Rugby, Warwks, CV21 3BX   *Tel:* 0788 78328/9.

Cruse (bereavement)
126 Sheen Road, Richmond, Surrey TW9 1UR   *Tel:* 081 940 4818.

Westminster Pastoral Foundation
23 Kensington Square, London W8   *Tel:* 071 937 6956, 071 376 2404/5

Advice and support groups for HIV and AIDS
The London Lighthouse
Residential and support centre for people living with HIV, ARC and AIDS
111–117 Lancaster Road, London W11 1QT   *Tel:* 071 792 1200, ext. 2115

The Terence Higgins Trust
The main UK charity dealing with HIV and AIDS: support groups, counselling, legal advice, grants, education and information
52–54 Grays Inn Road, London WC1X 8LT   *Tel:* 071 831 0330
Helpline: 071 242 1010

National Helpline: 0800 567 123
Offers advice, information and referrals on any aspect of HIV or AIDS. All calls free, line open 24 hours a day.

Index

gifted hands 64–7
gifts, psychic 64–73
God
  agent of all healing 23, 26–7, 31–2,
    37–8, 116, 126–7
  receiving of Holy Spirit 88–9
  praying to 15, 79–81, 83, 85–7
Grayshon, Jane 114
  A Pathway through Pain 115, 116
group healing 15, 85 *see also* prayer:
  groups

hair analysis 100
handicaps 31–2, 122–4
hands, gifted 64–7
harmony 21–4 *see also* wholeness
healers 8–9, 34, 60, 70, 73, 76
healing 8–10, 33–4
  centres 12–13, 153
  ministries 11, 14–15, 37, 142
  services 15, 87–8, 89
  types of
    alternative therapies 98–101
    charismatic 14, 71, 88–9
    curative 33–4, 36
    deliverance 14–15, 68, 91–2
    faith 8, 10–15, 73–8
    natural 43–53
    self 101–2
    spiritual 12, 46, 58–9, 78–89,
     112, 126–7
     sacraments 89–90
    through psychic sensitivity 68,
     69, 72
    through touch 64–7, 100–1
health 6–8, 33, 97, 129–32
  alternative medicine 54–60
herbal medicine 10, 99
holistic medicine 29–30 *see also*
  wholeness
Holy Communion 90
Holy Unction, sacrament of 90
homeopathic medicine 99

Israel, Dr Martin 72–3, 141–2

Jenkins, David (Bishop of Durham)
  6, 7, 8
Jesus Christ 11, 85

Kerin, Dorothy 12–13, 141
kinesiology 99
Kyle, William 142

Larcombe, Jennifer Rees 81–2, 84,
  104, 133
laying on of hands 12, 59, 87–8
Lembede, Anton 22–3
London Lighthouse 118
Lourdes 11–12, 77

McGilvray, Dr James 7
MacNutt, Francis 14
Masham, Lady 113
massage 100–1
Mayne, Michael 104–6
meditation 43, 44 *see also*
  transcendental meditation
miracles 11–12, 43

Nagai, Dr 38–41, 141
nature
  co-operation with 53–60
  healing rhythms 42–53
Nolan, Christy 113

opposites
  co-existence of 48–9
original sin 27
orthodox medicine 9, 29, 97
osteopathy 99

Paré Dr Ambroise 32
Paul, St 25, 26, 125
physics, quantum 45–6
Pietroni, Patrick
  The Greening of Medicine 98–9
Pincott, Christine 85–6
polarity 46–50
Polkinghorne, John
  Science and Creation 48, 50
Potts, Harry 37
prayer 43, 46, 58–9, 60, 78–9, 87, 112
  126–7
praying 79–83, 83–9
psychic sensitivity 62–73
psychology 15–16

Quakers 89